CELEBRATE WITH Sprinkles

BRITTANY YOUNG

HARVEST HOUSE PUBLISHERS
EUGENE, OREGON

I was raised watching my sweet grandmother intentionally celebrate all those around her. From neighbors to church friends and pastors to people she encountered...everyone received her warmth and hospitality. Mamaw Joyce ingrained in me that this is how you do life—bless those around you in whatever small yet heartfelt way you can. Before we ever put the words "Certified Celebrator" together, my grandmother was laying the foundation upon which we are still building today.

Contents

THE JOY OF INTENTIONAL CELEBRATION

Sprinkles are happy. They just are. Add a few to a store-bought cupcake or a Sunday morning pancake, and you've got a party on your plate. So why don't we dress up simple basics and celebrate life and loved ones more often?

The answer for most women is the same: *I already pack so much into a day. I'm not sure I can host parties... even if that sounds like a happy addition.* If you're a mom, you are a manager, caregiver, cook, entertainer, chauffer, referee, nurse, teacher, decorator, and wiper of tears. I have been right where you are (who are we kidding—I still am!) with so many responsibilities to juggle that I drop the joy without realizing it.

Well, a few years ago, I noticed. Then I decided to shine a light on the simple moments that deserve a few sprinkles. I started sharing tips and building a community of kindred spirits. Soon I called myself a Certified Celebrator and kept the party going.

You are one of those kindred spirits. When you saw the words *celebrate* and *sprinkle*, I bet you started to imagine braided streamers, pink icing, and twinkle lights. Or whatever your version of a happy place is. I knew I liked you.

I'm no artist or chef, but I am a crafty mama who likes to honor everyday moments, casual Saturdays, highlights in my family's life, girlfriends who keep me sane, and gatherings that draw all ages together. Are you with me?

I've got pretty. I've got practical. I've got your back.

Sprinkles—the sugary, confetti kind—are just the beginning. The secret to a successful party is to sprinkle extras throughout the party's theme, decorations, treats, craft offerings, activities, and welcoming touches. When you host, simply pick and choose where you go the extra smile. In the pages that follow, I provide lots of lovely photos, ideas, and inspiration:

- 20 themed parties that are versatile (Girl, most holiday ideas can be used year-round.)
- Simple DIYs, craft projects, and tablescape decor creations
- Halfway-Homemade recipes and doable gala goodies (Doable never means dull.)
- Decor with more—more color, more creativity, more flexibility, more happy
- No-fret activities with age-friendly suggestions
- Easy and beautiful gifts and party favors
- Tips for smooth and personal party planning
- Sprinkle in the Special—extras that accelerate the celebration factor

Do yourself a party-planning favor and take a deep breath. Kiss goodbye those desperate hours of scrolling through Pinterest the night before you're hosting. Sit back, grab one of those sprinkle-sensational cupcakes, attend these parties, and start planning your own.

Certified Celebrator Party Closet

People often ask what's in my craft and party closet because I'm all about using what's on hand and dressing up the basics again and again. You might not need the stash that I've accumulated; however, you're a wise woman who wants the basics on hand to save time and your budget throughout the year.

Here are my top five gotta-have-'em faves:

1. Balloons and streamers
2. Variety of jar sizes (pack with snacks, toys, utensils, or door prizes)
3. Cake stands, trays, and serving bowls (to serve goodies and to add variety to your table)
4. Disposable plates, bowls, and cups
5. Colorful scrapbook paper

Bonus item: sprinkles, of course!

I know...simple as can be. But I promise y'all, this really is all one needs to dress up any room or setting. Last-minute party plans? No problem!

What to Celebrate?

Oh, my favorite topic. My list of reasons, excuses, and people to celebrate goes on and on. (I *am* the one who considers fancifying a flapjack a mini celebration.) Maybe you just received a reminder text that you're hosting youth group... tonight! Or you've committed to throwing a party for your daughter's eighth-grade graduation or your brother-in-law's fiftieth birthday. With this treasury of ideas, you can say yes to hosting without regret and with excitement.

In this pretty space, list ten reasons—including specific people—to celebrate this year. If you get stuck, no worries. By the time you have savored the first few parties, the ideas will start flowing. And once you start hosting in simple and intentional ways, you'll catch the party fever.

1. _____

2. _____

3. _____

4. _____

5. _____

6. _____

7. _____

8. _____

9. _____

10. _____

Brittany's Dozen—Party Planning Guide

Here is the basic order in which I coordinate the details for a party. Let's say I have decided to host a party for a few neighbors and friends. These are the 12 steps or choices that get me from "Hmm, I am ready to plan a party" to P-Day with a genuine smile (and not a stress grimace).

1. **Decide the reason for the party.** And if that reason is a guest of honor, check with that person for possible dates and times.

2. **Set details.** Think through the basics: date, time, location.

3. **Create the guest list.**

4. **Determine your budget.**

5. **Decide your theme.**

6. **Invite the people.**

7. **Create your team.** One person can't do it all. If you have friends who are super talented, use their gifts. Most will be honored you asked for their help.

8. **Determine the entertainment.** Outdoor games, swimming party, magician, dance party...start thinking about what people will do while they are there, and take care of any last needs.

9. **Create your shopping list.** You will likely have two lists: groceries and craft/home decor supplies. Purchase craft items as early as a week or two before the date. Shop for groceries two days before so that you have one more day to grab anything you forgot.

10. **Arrange an advance craft session.** In advance of the party, make any of the DIYs or crafts you'll use as part of your decor or as a sample of the finished craft. That team you created? Invite them over for this prep party and enjoy a couple hours with snacks, music, and a couple friends or your kids. (You might start hosting parties so you can have the fun pre-party craft days.)

11. **Create a fun playlist.** Add to the mood of the party with a great soundtrack.

12. **Set up for the party.** Do this the night before or the morning of the event. Give yourself at least an hour to finish the last touches before people arrive so you can welcome them with ease and intention.

Confetti & Sprinkles

Let's start off our party quest the right way: I hereby dub you Confetti Queen. How does that feel? Are you reaching for your tiara? I hope so, because you and I are kicking off this celebration extravaganza in sparkly style.

Nothing invites your people to say "Let's party" quite like cascades of shimmery, glittery, colorful confetti. This gathering is a DIY ticker tape parade...in your home. So, who among your family and friends is ready to be celebrated in such a whimsical way? Whether you are honoring a birthday, graduation, or promotion, these ideas will spark smiles and serve up bliss.

With rainbows of sprinkles and swirls packed into every sweet treat and creative craft, this is sure to be a sensational soiree.

PARTY POSSIBILITIES

Confetti doesn't have to be confined to just one celebration. I declare that any party, any day, for any reason will benefit from billows of happy, colorful confetti clouds. Is a friend having a milestone birthday? Is your spouse starting a new job? Did your daughter get a part in the school play? Is your son in his first piano recital? Start spreading the joy and showering someone special.

A Visual Feast of Color

Color and shimmer are the stars of this show. Set up your confetti in a specific area on a tabletop, counter, or even bar cart. (If littles are present, designate separate spaces for the confetti and snacks so the kiddos don't confuse sparkles for snacks.) Invite your guests to create their own color mixes and combinations.

Utilize crafts made ahead of time as part of your decor to show what this confetti is capable of! Depending on what word or letters you chose, that might be a cute accent inside a wreath on your front door as guests arrive! Tall letters that can stand would provide some height on your tablescape as well. Color-Wave Wands can be displayed like flowers when placed in a tall vase.

All of your decor and setup can shine with simple touches. (No magic wand required, though the Color-Wave Wand is pretty special!) Consider adding string lights, glitter Play-Doh creations, foil garlands to reflect the joyful glow, etc.

SPRINKLE IN THE SPECIAL

Invite guests to create to-go confetti cones as a cute takeaway from the event. It's easy. Take a piece of scrapbook or cardstock paper, create a cone shape by rolling one corner to the opposite corner, secure in place along the edge with glue or tape. Fill with homemade or purchased confetti!

tip If you plan to have guests throw confetti during the event, think ahead about space and cleanup. Though it does make a beautiful mess, flooring surfaces like hardwood, tile, or linoleum will allow for simpler cleanup!

tip Keep confetti in a cute and tidy display. Clear jars showcase the happy and rein in the unexpected showers of shimmer. When the party ends, simply pour each jar's leftovers into a Ziploc bag for easy access when the next celebration arises.

Word Wow

Take a wooden letter or word from blah to oooo-la-la! Have guests create monograms, full names, or inspiration words. This is the alpha-better choice for a craft!

ALL YOU'LL NEED: craft store wooden words or letters, Mod Podge, sprinkles

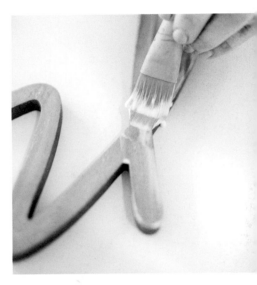

1. Show the guests how to quickly apply a thin coat of Mod Podge to the first letter. If their pieces are large, have them do a section at a time so the Mod Podge doesn't dry before they're finished.

2. Sprinkle confetti onto the same area until achieving the desired amount of coverage.

3. Repeat with each letter and let dry. Have everyone share their works of word art.

4. If your family is participating, have each member decorate a couple versions of the first letter of their name. Place these as decor accessories in special places: mantels, bookshelves, bedroom doors, dining table as a centerpiece, windowsills, bedside tables, etc.

tip
For a lighter option, you can find papier-mâché letters in many craft or fabric stores.

Color-Wave Wand

Gather everyone around a craft table. Even the tiniest tikes can join in on this colorful project that gives tissue paper a magical makeover.

ALL YOU'LL NEED: tissue paper in a rainbow of colors, double-sided tape, dowel rods

1. Fold the tissue paper the long way (hot dog style).

2. Layer multiple colors if desired.

3. Cut one-inch strips from the loose edge to within an inch of the folded base.

4. Wrap double-sided tape around the tip of a small dowel rod.

5. Attach it to the beginning of your tissue paper at the folded side.

6. Add a piece of double-sided tape on the folded edge of tissue every couple of inches so it will stick as you roll the dowel rod up into the tissue paper.

7. Secure with tape at the end, and let the celebration begin!

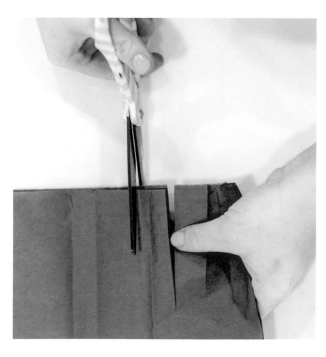

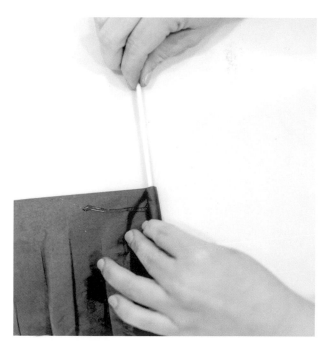

Pretty Party Platters

Serve up smiles with confetti platters.

ALL YOU'LL NEED: Mod Podge, a clear glass or acrylic dish or platter, confetti

1. Working by sections, apply a thin coat of Mod Podge to the bottom side of the dish.

2. Top the glue with a sprinkling of confetti before it dries.

3. Let dry, then flip over and use to serve up some shimmer.

 tip To clean these trays, wipe down with a damp cloth. If you only decorate the underside of the tray, it is food safe. Do not microwave.

Confetti Candy Melts

So simple. So sweet!

- White candy melts
- Pink candy melts
- Blue candy melts
- Purple candy melts
- Coconut oil
- Parchment paper
- Variety of sprinkles

Place half of each bag of colored melts into a separate small bowl. Add ½ teaspoon coconut oil to each bowl. Microwave the candy melts as directed on the package until smooth. Cover your baking sheet with parchment paper. Drop spoonfuls of the candy melts in a random color arrangement onto the parchment paper. Swirl the colors together with a spoon, knife, or skewer. Don't overmix so the swirls will stay pretty. Before the candy melts, cool and then add the sprinkles. Refrigerate for 45 minutes or until hardened.

Fruity Fun Parfait

Pile on the smiles with every spoonful of this yummy yogurt parfait!

- Fresh fruit
- Yogurt
- Granola
- Sprinkles

Layer the ingredients, beginning with the yogurt, followed by fruit and granola, then top with sprinkles if you plan to serve immediately. If making a little ahead of time, layer only the yogurt and fruit, adding granola and sprinkles just before serving.

As an extra touch on the parfaits, simply stack strawberry slices on a skewer to create a gleeful little garnish!

Funfetti Trifle

Fun is built into each layer of this tasty trifle.

CAKE

- 1 box vanilla cake mix
- 4 eggs
- 1 cup butter, melted
- 1 cup milk
- ½ cup multicolored sprinkles

FILLING

- 2 cups milk
- ½ cup powdered sugar
- 2 (3.4 oz.) boxes white chocolate pudding mix
- 1 (16 oz.) container whipped topping
- Additional sprinkles to top it off

DIRECTIONS FOR THE CAKE

Grease a 9 x 13-inch pan. Mix the cake mix with the eggs, butter, and milk in a large bowl. Whisk for 2 minutes or mix with an electric mixer. Stir in the sprinkles and pour into the pan. Bake according to the directions on the box. Set aside to cool.

DIRECTIONS FOR THE FILLING

Mix milk and powdered sugar together until the sugar dissolves. Add the pudding mix and set aside for a few minutes. Fold in the whipped topping and place in the refrigerator. Once the cake is cool, cut it into large cubes and line the bottom of a trifle bowl or apothecary jar. Top with the filling and repeat the layers. Cover the last layer of filling with rainbow sprinkles. Refrigerate and serve.

Happy Bee-Day

Parties are extra sweet when you're planning and preparing for a special someone's birthday. As a queen bee of hostessing, you'll make this gathering a buzzworthy event. Regardless of which bee-day your guest of honor is celebrating, this theme is flexible and will fly alongside any guest of honor. Wouldn't this be fabulous for a daughter or niece's sweet 16 party or bridal shower? You could add some bee-dazzle sparkle here and there and have leis and temporary floral tattoos.

I have plenty of ideas for decor touches that won't sting your budget. Your guests will be abuzz with joy as they soak up the clever details and flit from yummy treats to creative crafts. So, invite the swarm over to the hive 'cause this shindig is golden. I'm showcasing honeybees, bumblebees, and the *A*'s, *Bee*s, and *C*'s of doing a party right.

No birthday to celebrate on the horizon but you're ready to sing "Let there be bees on earth"? The reasons to use this theme soar beyond bee-days to all days, gatherings, and moments when you want to serve your happy colony the nectar of good cheer.

PARTY POSSIBILITIES

So many ideas! Here are three from my top-hive. Beyond the bee-day theme, this is a fun honey-do bridal shower party where the guests are invited to help a bride-to-be create a "honey do this" list for her future hubby. Host this for a friend from the office and call it a worker-bee party. Or gather your women's prayer group or reading group with invitations rejoicing in Proverbs 16:24: "Gracious words are a honeycomb, sweet to the soul and healing to the bones."

I can't help myself. Other celebrations to bless with this clever presentation include a bumblebee baby shower or a spring kickoff with your gardening gal pals.

Decor to Bee Admired

Make a stunning impression with your decor arrangement. Feature the Donut-Hole Hive and Bumble Layer Cake as a collective centerpiece on your tablescape. Scatter a few finished beehive buckets and honeypots to hold utensils or fresh flowers.

Highlight a variety of yellow tones and fresh flowers. I love the visual balance of the geometric honeycombs combined with the free-form shapes of the flowers and fixin's. For a little extra shimmer and shine, add gold to your color scheme.

tip Vary the height of items in your space to create a more interesting tablescape. Toss in taller vases with long stems to achieve more height. Another option would be to stack the buckets or pails bottom to bottom and top to top to increase their peak.

Honeycomb Hexagons

Turn the focus to a themed craft if you're hosting a younger colony of bee-day partygoers. These honeycombs are such a fun, festive feature that some might call them the bee's knees. Make a couple in advance so your guests have an example and you have another decoration.

ALL YOU'LL NEED: cardstock bases, Popsicle sticks, hot glue gun, adornments

1. Create a hexagon design on a piece of cardstock as a template to go by.

2. Place Popsicle sticks on the design and glue into place.

3. Overlap the top of one with the bottom of another.

4. Overlap the sides of multiple pieces to form a larger honeycomb formation and let dry.

5. Top with a plastic honeybee or other adornments.

Honeypots

What's better than a cupcake holder painted like a honeypot? And, it's as easy as 1, 2, 3!

1. Paint the rim and surrounding area of a terra-cotta pot with yellow paint. Make this semi-messy so it looks like dripping honey.

2. Write the word *honey* in Sharpie on the side.

3. Place a cupcake inside for a sweet surprise.

Beehive Buckets

Need a place to store your nectar? Put these pails on your in-advance project list.

1. Pick up some small yellow pails (or plain ones to spray paint) at your craft or dollar store.

2. Wrap twine around the pail to give the layered look of a hive.

3. Add bumblebee stickers as a final touch.

Donut-Hole Hive

Let hungry guests dive into this tall stack of delicious donuts. You'd be right to officially call this a not-at-all homemade hive (though it did take a lot of effort to resist eating all of these while I stacked them in the shape of a beehive).

Bee-nana Pudding

Break tradition and garnish this dish with honeycomb cereal bites.

- 2 (5.9 oz.) packages French vanilla pudding
- 1 (8 oz.) container sour cream
- 1 can sweetened condensed milk
- Sliced bananas
- Honeycomb cereal

Prepare the French vanilla pudding per the directions. Blend in the sour cream and sweetened condensed milk. Spoon into individual containers, and top with the sliced bananas and honeycomb cereal bites.

SPRINKLE IN THE SPECIAL

Give your guest of honor a special gold crown and dub her Queen Bee of the gathering. Send her home with a honeycomb weave basket filled with different varieties of honeys, teas, and sweets.

Swarm Salad

This salad is filled with fruits and proteins and will delight and refresh girlfriends or parents when you are hosting an all-ages gathering. It can be a sophisticated touch for that bridal shower too.

- Arugula lettuce
- Rotisserie chicken, removed from bone
- Diced apples
- Dried fruit

- Nut of choice
- Feta cheese
- Dressing: apple cider vinegar, honey, pepper

Wash and tear the lettuce, and then put it in a bowl. Add the pieces of chicken and sprinkle with the apples, dried fruit, nuts, and cheese. Drizzle with dressing and enjoy.

Bumble Layer Cake

Before anyone takes flight for their home hive, be sure they get a slice of this halfway-homemade bumble cake.

- Grocery-store cake (naked or you can start with pre-frosted)
- 2 cans yellow buttercream frosting or vanilla with added yellow food coloring

Frost two naked grocery-store cakes with frosting of your choice. Stack one onto the other, and top with a fresh or fake sunflower bloom.

For the Love

Gather up the girls—it's a Galentine's Day party!

Invite your go-to gal pals to your home for a sensational scrapbooking, card-making session. Ladies can bring personal projects, extra embellishments to share, or a heart ready and willing to create something fun. This is a time to celebrate the love of laughter and fellowship. Single. Married. Engaged. Mending a broken heart. Any woman's love status is her ticket to appreciate and celebrate the gift of friendship.

From pretty-in-pink treats to crafts made to share with special someones, this party shares delight any time of year.

Decorations are super simple. You'll discover several inspirations in these pages. And don't forget to express *your* heart and style with any adorbs additions you have in mind. As the hostess with the mostess, check your stash and bust out any odds and ends that will add some color and sparkle. That red Christmas paper with silver sparkles could totally fit this theme. It's said that necessity is the mother of invention, so I'm thinking *creativity* is the daughter of invention, and she's *always* invited to my parties. Yours too, I bet.

Your gal gala will have a feast of sweets. Make the raspberry heart tarts, trifle, or sprinkle stacks in advance, or choose one or all of them to do with your friends.

PARTY POSSIBILITIES

The party is never really over. You know I like to revamp ideas for other celebrations and purposes. Utilize the ice-cream cone floral decor for other occasions such as summer birthday parties or a church ice-cream social or a Mother's Day brunch. Return to this theme and all its goodies for an engagement party or a bridal shower. If you, a special friend, or your parents are heading for a milestone anniversary, this party will fill all the hopes for that hurray.

Valentine Voilà Moment

Transform your dining table or buffet with a fabulous Valentine's Day tablescape. Bring the love with simple choices. Grab a clear hurricane vase or even a trusty apothecary jar. Gently place a regular ice-cream cone inside, then top with several pink roses for an outside-the-box bouquet accent or centerpiece. When you add a special touch like this, you offer a conversation piece and an inspiration piece. Sharing ideas that give other women joy is definitely one of my love languages.

tip Always consider what you already have before purchasing new items. Finding and using existing items in storage leaves room in your budget—and your closet—for other essentials or a few exciting items. What would you add with a few extra bucks? Another menu item, more craft options, additional decor? Or maybe a party petty cash fund for your next gathering. Like I said, the party is *never* over.

An adorable accent wall will really pop at this party. Use pink painter's tape to mark off the lines of a large tic-tac-toe board on your wall. Pick up some *X* and *O* balloons to complete a wall feature they will fall for.

This wall accent would be adorable at kids' birthday parties.

Pretty Place-Card Holders

Create a special place for your friends. Adorn your table with these easy-to-craft place-card holders.

ALL YOU'LL NEED: box of paper straws, hot glue gun

1. For each holder, you'll use two straws.

2. Fold one in half as your base.

3. Cut the other straw in half and use one of the pieces as the support for the back of the base.

4. Hot glue and pinch them together.

5. Fold the other half to create the holder on the front of your base.

6. Hot glue to secure.

 tip Place-card holders are clever mini easels useful at a wide variety of gatherings. I'm envisioning food labels at buffet-style tables, silent auction item description tags at a school/church event, recipe holders at a potluck, food allergy/ingredient displays for bake sales, etc. The possibilities are endless.

Hearts and Crafts Cards

If this kindred spirit gathering is in advance of Valentine's Day, the focus can be on making V-day cards. Then, keep the love growing by making cards to celebrate other personal occasions on the horizon.

What kind of card will you make? Something sentimental with a meaningful quote, song lyric, or shared memory? Are you going for humor, hoping to see a smile and share a giggle? Exchange ideas and suggestions; be each other's best resource. Gain inspiration from your favorite crafting blog or find unique ideas on Pinterest.

ALL YOU'LL NEED: supply of scrapbook paper, magazine cutouts, scissors, adhesive

Include all the imagination-freeing extras like glitter, stickers, and glitter pens.

The artistic creations don't have to be for a significant other. Think outside the boxed-card set and create cute notes for your kids, coworkers, baristas, or your parents.

Memory Making

Make the most of having all these inspiring supplies out of their craft containers. Invite your friends to create scrapbook pages. You can buy a package of Valentine-themed scrapbooking papers and accessories or just have some extra red or pink paper available.

This simple activity is relaxing. You'll wonder why you don't do this every week. Maybe you'll all make plans to do that very thing, because once your friends get to chatting and crafting, they won't want this afternoon to end. Neither will you.

SPRINKLE IN THE SPECIAL

In advance of the party, make or buy Valentine's Day cards for each friend who will be attending. Write a note sharing something you appreciate about each woman's heart. Take a moment during the gathering to pass these out.

SENTIMENTS FOR CARDS

Need a bit of inspiration? Here are a few quotes you can write on your cards. Or create a personal poem or sweet sentiment of your own.

A kiss makes the heart young again and wipes out the years.
RUPERT BROOK

You must allow me to tell you how ardently I admire and love you.
MR. DARCY, *PRIDE AND PREJUDICE*

A friend loves at all times.
PROVERBS 17:17

How do I love thee? Let me count the ways.
ELIZABETH BARRETT BROWNING

There is only one happiness in this life, to love and be loved.
GEORGE SAND

There is nothing I would not do for those who are really my friends. I have no notion of loving people by halves; it is not my nature.
ISABELLA THORPE, *NORTHANGER ABBEY*

My heart is ever at your service.
WILLIAM SHAKESPEARE

Love is patient, love is kind.
1 CORINTHIANS 13:4

Full-Heart Tarts

This homemade upgrade on a toaster pastry classic is so fun to put together.
Let your friends bake up some lovin' from the oven.

- 2 premade pie crusts
- 6 oz. raspberries
- 1 cup powdered sugar
- 1 T. water (more if icing is too thick to drizzle)
- Sprinkles

Preheat the oven to 350°. Cut the pie dough into an even number of hearts using a heart-shaped cookie cutter. Place half the dough hearts 2 inches apart atop the parchment paper on the baking sheet. Using a fork, gently poke 3 to 4 sets of small holes into the dough pieces. Spread 1 tablespoon of raspberries onto each heart. Place a second heart over the top. With the fork, lightly press the edges of the hearts together to make crimped edges. Poke 3 to 4 sets of holes on the top heart pieces. Bake the tarts for 15 minutes or until golden brown. In a small bowl, mix the powdered sugar with water to create icing to drizzle. Remove the tarts from the oven; drizzle the icing. Top with the sprinkles. Cool and serve.

Jars of Love Trifle

Layered with love, this gorgeous pastel dessert will have everyone oohing and ahhing and reveling in just how easy this is to create.

- 2 to 3 cups grocery-store bakery lemon cake cut into cubes
- Pink food coloring
- 1 (8 oz.) container whipped cream
- 2 cups strawberries
- Apothecary jars

Add a few drops of the food coloring to the whipped cream, and layer the ingredients into a clear apothecary jar. Easy peasy.

Sprinkle Stacks

As scrumptious as they are pretty, these stacks will please the appetites of every sweet tooth you know.

- Graham crackers
- Sliced strawberries
- Whipped cream
- Sprinkles
- Pink cotton candy

Stack your desired ingredients between two graham crackers and enjoy. And don't forget the sprinkles!

Book Club Social

There are all kinds of reasons we are hungry for simple and special parties and overwhelmed by bigger concepts. Some mamas are fraying at the edges, running from soccer games to piano recitals, and party hosting sounds like a far-off fantasy or another too-big responsibility. Others are intimidated by the process and panic before the invitations are purchased. For a gathering to happen, it needs to fit their comfort zone, not the crazy zone.

If this reflects the season you are living in or even the week you're having, I encourage you to consider the book club social. It has a clear focus, you can host at home or at a venue, and you can delegate to others any of the tasks, including making appetizers or leading the group discussion.

Besides, I bet you rock those readers! Am I right?

This theme is a welcoming blend of classic tale meets modern friendship novella. Reading never goes out of style because there is something for everyone on the written page. This party celebrates creativity, ideas, classics, the power of story, and the unique way books unite people—friends and strangers alike. It's a genuinely simple gathering that will prove to be an engaging page-turner.

PARTY POSSIBILITIES

Choose the book and then choose the location to meet. Gather the gang at your favorite coffee shop or local bakery. A small bookstore would probably welcome your sisters to their stacks. Strengthen the binding that holds your current friendships together, or start a new chapter surrounded by women with similar interests (faith, gardening, hiking, fiction). Kindred readers are a gift at any age.

Are your kiddos fascinated with fiction or fairy tales? Your friends-focused gathering might become the prologue to a junior club. Tell me the tweens wouldn't love a Harry Potter book club. You'll be encouraging reading, as well as supporting social interaction and communication with other kids. Sounds like a bestselling idea to me!

Decorate by the Book

Bring out your older hardcover books or newer ones with colorful, pretty bindings and turn them into your go-to accessories. If you don't have any that suit your preferred color theme, head to a thrift store or used book store and gather some goodies. Set your finds under vases or other decor elements. Stack them, lean them, or stand them on your shelves if you host this at home.

For the ideas in this section, you can use loose pages from a book that has a broken binding or buy packets of pages from a vintage store.

I have a book-page wreath in my regular home decor, so I took it with me to the cute little bakery that welcomed our group to gather. See what you have at home that is easy to transport to a different location if you have chosen not to host at home. A centerpiece that suits the theme will make the event more memorable and beautiful.

 tip Have a couple newer books or loose pages you want to give a vintage look to? Stain them with coffee. It creates the perfect aged-sepia tone. Consider doing this to any invitations if you decide to send hard-copy party details.

SPRINKLE IN THE SPECIAL

Have a special book among your decor pieces that you plan to give away as a door prize? Maybe it is a vintage book on friendship from the thrift store or a colorful coffee-table book on gardens. If you have time, make a special floral bookmark to go with the door prize.

Word-Wrap Vase

Club members won't be the only ones getting wrapped up in the reading! This reader-worthy vase can be used to reflect the theme in your decor or to have as a giveaway to fellow club members.

ALL YOU'LL NEED: vase(s), loose book pages, hot glue gun

1. Create a line of hot glue down the left and right edge of the page.

2. Press quickly onto your vase.

3. Decide how much overlap you prefer.

4. Repeat with the next page until your vase is covered.

Floral Bookmark

Before you exchange notes on your latest reads, save a spot for a bookmark DIY.

ALL YOU'LL NEED: small faux flowers, Popsicle sticks, hot glue gun

1. Snip the small faux flower at its base.

2. Attach it to the Popsicle stick with hot glue.

3. Allow to cool.

Storybook Blooms

Blooms tucked into paper-wrapped vases make adorable centerpieces. The plot of pretty thickens as the theme carries over to centerpieces made from book pages.

This is so easy and fun to make in advance of the party. Your friends will love it. Cut a circle of paper into a spiral. Beginning at the center, roll the paper into a budding flower, gluing as you go. Add petals of paper until you reach the desired size.

Ready...Set...Read... Baked Brie

This looks elegant and fancy but is actually easy and fast, and there's nothing fictional about that.

- Brie wheel
- Pepper jelly
- Pretzels, crackers, or veggies

Bake the Brie as directed. Spread onto pretzel, crackers, or veggies; spoon pepper jelly on top; and serve.

Pepper Jack Pesto Panini

These meatless minis are bursting with flavor. The pepper jack pesto combination really packs the perfect punch for book club brunch with your besties.

- Pepper jack cheese
- Tomato slices
- Store-bought pesto
- 1 loaf Italian bread, sliced

On a cookie sheet or two, distribute the slices of bread. Add pepper jack cheese to half of them. Toast in the oven. Remove the bread from the oven when it is crunchy-delicious, and add tomatoes on top of the cheese. Dollop on a spoonful of pesto and top with a plain slice of toasted bread.

Garden Basil Bites

A simple yet elegant appetizer to enjoy while you chat about the most recent chapters!

- Apple slices
- 1 (8 oz.) container garden herb cream cheese
- Bacon, cooked to preferred crispness
- Fresh basil leaves

Tuck an apple slice under a piece of basil. Add a bit of garden cream cheese spread. Top with bacon crumbles.

BOOK GROUP CHAT QUESTIONS

1. What part of the story or message captured your attention?

2. If the book's author or main character was attending an event at your house, what kind of gathering would you plan?

3. If you were to rewrite any of the book, what would you change and why?

4. How do you make room for reading in your life?

5. How does reading make you feel?

6. Is this a book you will pass along to others now that you're done? Why or why not?

Ice Cream for BREAKFAST

Break a few rules and traditions with a breakfast spread everyone will scream for. Your littles will be pinching themselves to make sure they're not sleepwalking into their greatest fantasy: ice cream for breakfast! (I confess, this still is my fantasy.) Spread out your bountiful buffet of tasty toppings. Decisions, decisions. Your cuties will be toasting Mom by clinking their glasses of milk and grinning with melt-your-heart smiles.

Even if ice cream is not your tinies' fantasy (more like a bellyache waiting to happen), they can enjoy their own smorgasbord of summer sweets. Colorful cotton candy, their favorite fun-sized candy bars, or a personal cupcake are a few options that could top their breakfast cones.

Living life with joy à la mode is the sweetest treat you can share with your family, friends, and youngins. Sweet dreams are made of this.

PARTY POSSIBILITIES

Waffling back and forth about when to use this theme? What kid under the age of 100 wouldn't love this for a birthday party? Start or end your summer or welcome a child home from camp with this dairy delight. Or join with some area parents to host a big ice-cream block party for neighborhood kids on the first day of summer. If you've had a *Frozen* movie-themed slumber party for a gaggle of girls, this breakfast the next morning is a must.

All Things Scream Ice Cream

It's a happy affair with ice cream everywhere! Eat it. Decorate with it. Adorn your walls with it. Well, okay. I don't mean to literally spread mint chip scoops on your walls. (Though the kids might do this for ya!) I mean, bring on the ice-cream-cone zone with every decor touch. These ideas are simple, lively, and entertaining to create in advance and enjoy during the party.

I am a happy woman when food is so pretty that it's baked-in decor. A tall stack of pancakes is an edible centerpiece for each place setting. And the guests get to decorate it with gorgeous and delicious toppings. You could say they get to stack it in their flavor!

Carnations are lovely and long-lasting, which make them the perfect flower for party tablescapes. Let ice-cream cones double as vases and place the carnations inside. Add a red carnation in the center to transform this floral decor into the image of an ice-cream sundae creation. These beauties will last through your event.

Sugary Sweet Scene

This party element offers a double scoop of fun: one part decoration and one part game (if you want to churn out even more laughter). The game details will follow.

ALL YOU'LL NEED: pink painter's tape, multiple pastel shades of honeycomb tissue balls, red tissue paper or pom-pom—that's it!

1. Use pink painter's tape to create the V-shape of a cone on the wall.

2. Add crisscross stripes to form the cone texture.

3. Create scoops from decorative honeycomb tissue balls.

4. Fluff up a variety of sizes, and then tape them to the wall cone.

5. Top it all with a red tissue puff or pom-pom as the perfect cherry.

6. Don't forget the sundae social photo ops in front of this colorful, dimensional backdrop.

Cherry-on-Top Game

You can hold off on adding the red pom-pom to your wall cone masterpiece and turn "cherry on top" into a call for fun and games. Blindfold a guest, spin them around, then hand them a red pom-pom with tape or poster putty on one side. Have them do their best to place the cheery cherry atop the wall cone. Give a prize to the winner—such as an apothecary jar filled with ice-cream sundae toppings. Plan the placement of the design to be sure people can reach the top of the cone.

Dipped Peanut Butter Cookies

Elevate a favorite!

- 1 (16 oz.) package peanut butter cookies
- 1 (12 oz.) package white chocolate candy melts
- Red cinnamon candy or pink chocolate hard shell candy
- Sprinkles (of course!)

Warm up the white chocolate melts per package instructions. Dip the cookies partway in the chocolate. Decorate with sprinkles and candy.

SPRINKLE IN THE SPECIAL

I positively adore apothecary jars. They are multitasking decor pieces that give your home and guests a large scoop of special. Create a treat jar with waffle cones or cookies and ideas for making yummy ice-cream sandwiches. Have one made up with all the cone delights and use it as a door or game prize.

Cereals-ly Yummy Bars

Choose cereals that are colorful!

- 2 T. unsalted butter
- 8 cups mini marshmallows
- 6 cups cereal

Grease a 9 x 13-inch pan (large, deep, nonstick works best!), and set to the side.

In a different pan and over low heat, melt the butter and 6 cups of the mini marshmallows in another pan until completely melted. Remove from the heat and stir in the cereal plus the remaining 2 cups of mini marshmallows. Keep stirring until all the cereal and marshmallows are coated and combined. Pour the mixture into the prepared pan. Press and spread to fill to all corners of the pan.

Allow to cool before serving.

tip If you are using your hands to press the cereal bar mixture into the pan, coat them with baking spray or butter so the mix doesn't stick to your hands.

Ice-Cream Sprinkle Sandwiches

A spin on traditional cookies and cream.

- Butter cookies (or your favorite flavor)
- Vanilla ice cream
- Sprinkles

Scoop vanilla ice cream between two prepared butter cookies. Roll them in sprinkles. Serve!

Here's the Scoop

Too cute and too easy!

- Paper doilies
- Ice-cream cones
- Cupcakes (premade or homemade)
- Jar of cherries

Wrap ice-cream cones in paper doilies. Set the cupcake inside the opening of the cone for an appealing presentation! Cherries on top complete the vision.

Bunny Kisses & Easter Wishes

Let's not become so overrun with routine that important occasions go by without the recognition they deserve. "The year Mom forgot my Easter basket" is not the memory you want your child to recall. I won't let that happen. Host a spring gathering for your peeps like a celebration eggspert with these simple tips, tricks, and recipes.

This party sprouts inspiration with engaging activities and DIYs suitable for all ages. I always keep you and your ever-precious time and resources in mind. Decor is designed to bloom from the basic elements, and all menu items come together quick and *cheep*. By the way, the resulting goodies will have everyone clucking for more. I promise!

Host this color-dipped celebration after Easter Sunday service or anytime during this season of beginnings and beauty. You'll be glad you took time to plant the seeds of possibility and let this party blossom with cheer for those you hold dear. Look, I'm rhyming...that's how inspiring this party is.

Let's get cracking.

PARTY POSSIBILITIES

You can utilize these ideas to simply celebrate Spring—the season of renewal and growth can be honored without the eggs and bunnies. Invite friends over to plant some seeds or bulbs in painted planters or in a section of your yard. When this friendship garden is overflowing with blossoms and promising sprigs of green, you will celebrate the gift of those people all over again. Consider other features like the centerpiece design as inspiration for a gardening club or garden party get-together.

Decorating Choice to Rejoice

Need some inspiration for your Easter tablescape? Fragrant blooms edge our lawns and invite us to stop and rejoice in creation's renewal. Your party decorations can do the same for your guests. Take a walk on the fresh side and showcase food as part of this gathering's theme. Decorating for this occasion is as easy as hip, hop, hooray!

To complement the natural centerpiece, add some graceful tulips atop a foundation of hard-boiled eggs. Leave the oval beauties *au naturel* for a crisp, clean look, or let your littles dye the batch of eggs before adding them to the basket for a happy nod to an Easter tradition.

Create your own Easter egg trophies. Simply glue plastic eggs to inexpensive trophies.

Bunny Party Hats

Heelllloooo! Party hats aren't just for birthdays. Give any fete a signature headpiece.

All you'll need are a few items you likely have left over from previous parties: party hats, scrapbook or construction paper, pencil, scissors, glue, and pom-poms

1. Draw bunny ears onto the scrapbook paper and cut them out.

2. If party hats don't suit your colors or theme, cover them with construction paper and secure it.

3. Glue the ears onto the sides of the party hats.

Pssst...this would make a perfect craft to occupy the kiddos while the adults hide the Easter eggs. Once the hats are done, be sure to get every-bunny together for a photo hop.

SPRINKLE IN THE SPECIAL

Send guests home with the promise of renewal. Place several floral bulbs in a small paper sack or mesh pouch and tie it with twine or ribbons. Attach an inspirational phrase or verse.

The old is gone, the new is here!
2 CORINTHIANS 5:17

Let us rejoice today and be glad.
PSALM 118:24

His mercies begin afresh each morning.
LAMENTATIONS 3:23 NLT

Cabbage Centerpiece

Create a cabbage floral piece by arranging flowers to rest inside a head of cabbage, or wrap collard greens around your plain vase to kick up the color. First, peel back a few of the outer cabbage leaves. Hollow out the center enough that a small mason jar or piece of floral foam will fit. Next, arrange your stems in a bundle. Finally, add filler so the jar or foam remains hidden.

The blooms and natural greenery breathe life into your decor. Who knew cabbage could be stylish and captivating? Now the secret's out, and your guests will *leaf* with new ideas for their own homes.

 tip If you take the party outdoors, set up the patio table on the lawn and sprinkle the Easter eggs atop the green grass surrounding your celebration station. In advance of the gathering day, poll your favorite peeps and create an Easter/Spring family bucket list of foods and activities that everyone will enjoy.

Confetti Easter Eggs

Nothing says party like confetti. And *everything* is better with a little bling, right? Whether you are looking for a unique way for the littles to decorate their eggs or interested in a fun craft to bring a little sparkle to your Easter decor and tablescape, this is eggs-actly what will keep your group hopping happy.

ALL YOU'LL NEED: paintbrushes, Mod Podge, plastic or papier-mâché eggs, confetti, paper plate

1. Brush Mod Podge onto the eggs.

2. Sprinkle confetti onto the eggs before the glue dries.

3. Arrange the eggs in your decor or in baskets.

 tip Place a paper plate under the eggs before sprinkling so you catch any extra confetti.

Easter Brunch Punch

Serve up something extra special this holiday. Colorful beverages always make an event feel special.

- 1 (12 oz.) can frozen pineapple juice
- 8 cups pineapple juice
- 1 pint raspberries
- Round pineapple slices
- 8 to 10 scoops rainbow sherbet
- 2 liters Sprite

Combine ingredients, chill, and enjoy!

Bunny Hop Pops

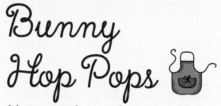

It's a no-melt miracle. Your minis can enjoy these while crafting party hats or hunting for eggs without the worry of melting or dripping onto their Easter outfits.

- 12 (.78 oz.) prepackaged Rice Krispy treats
- 1 cup white chocolate chips
- 1 cup shredded coconut
- Green food coloring
- Cake/cupcake embellishment

Melt the chips according to the package directions, and add a few drops of green food coloring. Dip the treats in melted chocolate and roll in coconut. Add embellishments.

Peeps Love Popcorn Treats

Little chicks will love these yummy treats full of popcorn deliciousness.

- 1 T. butter
- 20 large marshmallows
- 4 cups popcorn, popped

- 1 cup small graham crackers
- ¼ cup mini chocolate eggs
- 2 T. sprinkles

Spray an 8 x 8-inch baking pan with cooking oil. Melt the butter in a large bowl in the microwave for 45 seconds. Add the marshmallows, stir, and heat again for 1 minute. Stir the mixture, then add the popcorn and graham crackers. Transfer the mixture to the prepared pan and sporadically press the chocolate eggs on top, then add sprinkles. Allow the mixture to cool and harden for about 10 minutes. Slice and serve.

tip

Recipes for treat pops and popcorn bars can also be modified to fit any other season or holiday based on the ingredients you include.

Sip & Savor

You can't spell *party* without *tea*. Cordially invite your besties over for an elegant afternoon tea. Tickle their fancy with charming crafts and a delightfully delicious menu. May the chatter be witty and the decor royally grand as you connect or reminisce over tea and cookies.

Friends will savor every sip of tea and conversation when you draw them together around a beautiful table set with intention and an eye for detail. I need more moments surrounded by beauty and beautiful hearts. How about you?

In advance of this event, watch for teapots, cups, saucers, and the like at secondhand stores and antique shops. Don't be shy about asking around to see if friends have pieces you can borrow; they'll get an invitation in return. You don't have to have a complete matching tea set. An eclectic presentation of dishware and serveware creates a lovely blend of elegant and casual. Your guests will feel pampered the moment the tea is poured.

PARTY POSSIBILITIES

This theme is a great showcase for numerous occasions. Wouldn't it be lovely for a sip and see baby gender reveal party, a bridal shower, sweet 16 celebration, or a Mother's Day brunch? Honor a grandmother with a surprise tea for her, her friends, and your friends. Make it a legacy tea, and savor the connections between generations of women.

Perfect-to-a-Tea Decor

Embrace the shabby chic look of mismatched place settings with vintage elements such as scalloped edges, lace, florals, and faux pearls! Create a setting for all the senses. Soft music inspires an ambience as do fresh, fragrant flowers from the grocery store.

For a centerpiece, use a cake stand or stack up some pretty plates and encase them with a cake dome. If you don't have a cake stand, elevate your pieces by placing books beneath your tablecloth. This gives you lots of flexibility. Or bring out your collection of tea books and place them at varied heights on the table. Drape them with a doily to protect the covers before adding plates.

Mix solids with patterns and floral designs. Expect to be delighted by the unexpected. Don't forget that you can even find paper plates that look like little china saucers!

Interweave pieces and patterns, florals, solids, new, borrowed, etc.

Lace up your decor and elevate the elegance. Add touches of lace on walls, tables, and serving carts to create a lush and refined setting. For example, drape a lace tablecloth over the top of any solid color spread, and you have a rich foundation for your tea and treats spread. We'll look at more crafts and table extras that will please guests.

Flawless Floral Wreath

tip Check your craft stash for any extra
vine greenery left over from other
projects, or you may have some from a dated
piece that you could remove and revive!

When a project involves a hula hoop, you know it's about to be a splendidly good time. This wreath is easy peasy, y'a'll. (Stress is not served at this party!)

ALL YOU'LL NEED: a hula hoop, spray paint, faux flowers and vines, hot glue gun

1. Spray paint the hoop gold and allow it to dry.

2. Hot glue greenery to the surface of the hoop. Aim to cover a little more than half of the circle. (If you do a full wrap, the hoop won't rest flush against the wall.)

tip If you're investing some of your
budget in this project, the flowers are
where I would put the money. Get a few high-
quality blooms. They look incredibly real
these days. Find them on sale at Michaels or
Hobby Lobby.

3. Arrange the blooms into a cute little stack and hot glue them to the hoop. Add blooms of various sizes, and incorporate the colors that complement the party's pretty tones. Sensational!

Posh Party Hats

Disposable cups get a magical makeover in this dainty DIY! Entertain partygoers by inviting them to create their personal party hat while you steep the tea or finish welcoming your guests.

ALL YOU'LL NEED: paper cups, artificial flowers, real lavender, trim from the craft store, hot glue gun

1. Choose a disposable cup in a color you like.

2. Turn the cup upside down and hot glue mini artificial flowers and small sprigs of lavender to the side.

3. Punch a hole on two sides of the cup and string ribbon through the holes to make the strap.

4. String a radiant ruffle around the rim of the cup.

SPRINKLE IN THE SPECIAL

Celebrate each guest and the bonds formed over the ritual of tea. Package together tea bags or homemade loose-leaf tea combinations and place in a small organza bag for each person.

Lovely Layered Cookies

Guests will love this sweet spin on tea sandwiches as pleasant pink icing is layered between satisfying slices of pound cake.

- Frozen pound cake
- Pink icing

Allow the pound cake to thaw, then slice it into ½-inch pieces. Pick a cute cookie cutter to shape the cake slices. Spread store-bought pink icing between two slices to create a delightful, sweet sandwich.

Tomato Caprese Salad

A toast! To the palate-pleasing taste achieved with next-to-no preparation and effort that pairs perfectly with tea and chatter among friends. You can even put this together as your guests mingle. Then pass the caprese, please.

- Cherry tomatoes
- Olive oil
- Salt and pepper
- Phyllo cups, baked
- Mozzarella cheese balls
- Fresh basil leaves
- Balsamic vinaigrette dressing

Preheat the oven to 375°. Roast the tomatoes in olive oil, salt, and pepper for about 35 minutes or until the tomatoes burst. This is the prime time to start stacking your ingredients. Set each tomato inside a phyllo cup, place one mozzarella ball and one fresh basil leave on top, and drizzle the stack with your favorite balsamic vinaigrette dressing.

Sip on Sereni-Tea

This refreshing twist on tea really hits the spot.

- Water
- Sugar
- Lavender buds
- Frozen lemonade
- Fresh lemon slices
- Food coloring (optional)

Combine ¾ cup water and ½ cup sugar in a saucepan. Bring to a low boil. Stir until the sugar dissolves, and then remove the pan from the heat. Add 3 to 4 lavender buds and allow the mixture to cool.

Prepare the frozen lemonade per the directions, minus 1 cup water. Remove the lavender buds from the sugar water in the saucepan, then pour the sugar water into the prepared lemonade. Add fresh slices of lemon.

For a lavender color (optional), add one drop of blue food coloring and one drop of red food coloring at a time, and stir until the desired color is achieved.

tip Your tea selection can be broad or simple. You can use individual flavors or large mixes. Have one decaffeinated offering.

Frozen Florals

Achieve effortless beauty in the smallest of details. These graceful ice cubes will quench the thirst and refresh the spirit of every guest. They are simple to make yet make a big impression.

Take tiny artificial florals and drop them into individual ice cube trays. (I adore these heart-shaped ones.) Pour water over the top and freeze. (Boiled water makes the clearest ice.) These delicate ice cubes are beautiful in pitchers of lemonade or ice water. If you want a natural version, add seasonal herbs or edible flowers instead of the plastic blooms.

Flamingo Fiesta

This event is nacho ordinary party! You are about to take taco night to the next level. Maybe you want to make your own sunshine on a rainy day, or you merely want a get-together with friends to get over a queso the Mondays. This could even be the kickoff to a stay-cation with sizzling style.

Whatever the reason you bring people together, here is all you'll need to manifest a fiesta in your home. Every bright and happy detail—from pink birds to painted pineapples—will have your guests thinking they've died and gone to paradise. I went south of the border and kept going with a flamboyance of Caribbean and South American flamingos and Latin American-inspired dishes.

Plan with the ease of a tropical breeze. The snacks are simple, and the decor is from the grocery store. Partygoers will pack their plates with pineapple pico and feast on the fresh fruit nachos. Anyone who tries to top this Flamingo Fiesta won't have a leg to stand on. And your best amigos will tacobout this relaxing and festive party for years to come. Olé!

PARTY POSSIBILITIES

Though the weather is always a factor, I adore any opportunity to move the party outside. If you aren't particularly crazy about pineapples, you could swap those for mini watermelons and still scoop out the inside and use these as flower vases. Pick your favorite one or two of these ideas, and just play up your usual taco Tuesday or maximize the theme for a bridal shower if the soon-to-be couple has a tropical honeymoon destination.

Pop with a Backdrop

A party's backdrop colors can amp up the first and lasting impressions. For this party, I shopped my own stash and chose black and white pieces to create a backdrop that allows the bright colors to shine. I used our gingham tablecloth, white serveware, cake stands, and so on. Flamingos and spray-painted pineapples add vibrant color and great textures.

Fresh flowers are something we like to include in every party and, really, in our everyday decor. These florals just seem to breathe life into the space. Be on the lookout for cute items on clearance as the seasons change. These precious pineapple drink cups were marked down to next to nothing, and I couldn't possibly pass them up. Now they are perfect as part of our Flamingo Fiesta!

Sweet Aloha Centerpiece

Put food at the center of your table, but this time as part of the decor! First, cut the top off the pineapple and scoop out the inside. Next, cut floral foam to fit. Arrange the stems and stick into the foam. Aloha!

tip Having basics in your party supply cupboard or closet or on your pantry shelf allows you to put together get-togethers without the stress. You will enjoy the freedom to extend full-color hospitality when someone needs celebrating right away. And that someone might be you!

Flamingos deliver the happy and humor to your party's decor. Let me tell you, you can snag cute flamingo decor pieces at thrift shops and discount stores now, and they can be utilized in any summer get-together. These quirky birds are the smile factor at this fiesta!

Your photo-fanatic friends will be fast fans of this ultimate umbrella backdrop. It shouts summer and sunshine. String several umbrellas into a garland strand by threading fishing line through the paper of the umbrellas, leaving space between. Zig-zag several strands to create a tropical summer backdrop.

SPRINKLE
IN THE SPECIAL

Because this fiesta is about flare and flash, create tropical vignettes anywhere you can. I set up a line of palm tree look-alikes behind the table. Another wave of beach-scene selfies coming up!

Pretty meets practical with this inexpensive table-topping, eye-popping decoration. Buy a few cans of brightly colored spray paint to match your party's color scheme. In a well-ventilated area, simply spray the pineapples until you reach your desired color. Allow them to dry completely before handling.

Piñatas—the Hit of the Party!

Bring on the energy and string up a piñata to entertain the kids if you are combining parents and children. Buy a premade piñata (or two), follow the instructions to fill it with tropical-flavored candies, and choose a safe place to hang it—either in a spacious room or in the yard.

tip If you have a variety of ages represented, give the older kids their own piñata, and let the younger kids have their fun with a piñata dangling at a height just for them.

Fresh Fruit Nachos

They will really value your friend-chip when these tasty tortillas hit their taste buds!

- Tortillas
- Vegetable oil
- Cinnamon
- Sugar
- Fresh fruit of choice
- Caramel or chocolate drizzle

Preheat the oven to 375°. Cut the tortillas into fourths or sixths to create chip pieces. Toss with vegetable oil. Sprinkle with cinnamon and sugar and then bake in a single layer for about 15 minutes or until toasted.

Top with your favorite fresh fruit and then drizzle with caramel or chocolate. Embellish however you like!

Did someone say ice cream? You bet. Add your favorite flavors for an extra dollop of yum.

Pineapple Pico

You won't shell out big pesos on this halfway-homemade upgrade to store-bought pico de gallo.

- Pico de gallo
- Pineapple (fresh or canned)
- 1 cup cilantro

Dice the pineapple. Add to the store-bought pico, plus a little juice. Stir in 1 cup cilantro. Serve chilled. Want even more color and flavor? Add chopped mango to the mix.

Quick Quesadillas

Your guests will be excited to be pooling around the kitchen waiting for these quesadillas to come out of the oven!

- 1 cup black beans
- 1 (8 oz.) block cream cheese, softened
- 1 cup cheddar cheese, shredded
- ½ cup diced jalapeños with juice
- Tortillas
- Tomatoes, diced

Preheat the oven to 375°. Combine the ingredients in the tortillas. Fold and bake until toasted and brown. Garnish with diced tomatoes.

Red, White & Boom

Let your freedom ring loud and clear! You are wonderfully made, and you are a gift to those around you. Your desire to sprinkle in the special for people you love is a brilliant one. Let that light shine through the wonder of all things floral and full of flare for the Fourth of July.

With the potential for noise and activity, take the party outside if you can so there's plenty of room for the red, white, and boom!

You are honoring Independence Day, so decorate and create your way. Give yourself the liberty to bust out the bar cart as a fun yet mobile organization unit for all things snap, crackle, pop. I'll show you how to decorate it in style so that when you park it in your front yard or on the porch, everyone will know where the spangled bash is happening.

Prepare a variety of fireworks from big booms to small sparklers. Whether you are indoors or outdoors, this party plan will brighten up anyone's night.

PARTY POSSIBILITIES

The neighbors won't fuss over the noise if they're part of the fun, so consider making this one a block party. Vacation Bible school participants would also have a blast at this gathering. And no worries if you take this indoors because of neighborhood or state rules, or you live in an apartment, or your plan for diamonds in the sky gets rained on. The fun will not fizzle! Flameless fireworks and party poppers all around. Set the holiday lights to twinkle mode. You can watch the fireworks on the big screen or break out crayons and glitter and let the brilliance of the littles steal the show.

Florals and Flares

This day's decorations and tablescapes welcome everyone and every style to the table. So toss in festive fabric, patriotic patterns, and rock-it ribbons. Jazz things up with some played-up pinwheels and pom-pom decor with stems stationed in a clear jar filled with mints. And get ready for some very festive ideas using fresh or faux flowers. All these could easily be used on indoor or outdoor tables and on serving surfaces.

Break out your bar or tea cart in disguise as a fun fireworks cart with all the fixin's! It's so easy to create a station that welcomes guests to come and see and enjoy the snacks or beverages. Littles will love the lights and sound of the cart and the sight of the treat cups made just for them. Have plenty of festive goodies like Pop Rocks and Firecracker Marshmallows they can snack on.

Organize fireworks from big booms to small snaps with clear apothecary jars. Such a pleasing display makes it easy to get the party started.

tip
If your neighbors, friends, or family have little ones, add plenty of safe sparkle to the party with flameless fireworks and plenty of extra party poppers. Double-check with parents if you are adding in sparklers. Create a hand protector for younger kids by poking a hole in a party cup and then threading the sparkler through.

Flower Flag

Get your Betsy Ross on. Bring fresh florals into the mix and create a floral flag that would delight the Founding Fathers...and mothers!

ALL YOU'LL NEED: mason jars, flowers in the colors of the flag

1. Gather up enough mason jars or other clear vessels to form a rectangle with an even number of rows.

2. Place the jars on a tray or board in case they need to be moved.

3. Fill each about half full of water.

4. Place blue flowers in the top left corner.

5. Then begin with a top red row as the first stripe and work your way down the rest of your flag. (If you have trouble finding a color, you can always go faux!)

Patriotic Planter

No green thumb is required for this lovely Fourth of July foolproof planter! But if you have a red, white, or blue one, you're made for this! Create several of these in advance for your decor, and have the supplies displayed and ready for a DIY activity for your guests, young or old.

ALL YOU'LL NEED: floral foam, flowerpots from a garden or craft store, flags of all sizes and styles, straw, moss, or flag-colored glass stones

1. Cut the floral foam to fit into the flowerpots.

2. Place the larger flags in the center of the foam.

3. Add the medium-sized flags around the larger ones.

4. Insert the tiny flags as a filler.

5. Cover the foam with straw, moss, or glass stones.

6. Guest-crafted decorations personalize the party, and then offer up party favors when it's time to say goodbye.

Homemade Party Poppers

Provide celebratory shimmer for guests at the party or at their home! These easy-to-make portable poppers are great parting gifts when it's time to say farewell.

ALL YOU'LL NEED: toilet paper rolls, balloons, scissors, tissue paper, glue gun or stick, pretty paper and washi tape options, confetti, and glitter!

1. Tie a balloon and snip just a smidge off the rounded end of the balloon.

2. Gently fit the open end of the balloon over an empty toilet paper roll.

3. Fill the roll with confetti and glitter.

4. With a thin layer of tissue paper, create a temporary top over the open end of the toilet paper roll.

5. Decorate the sides of the popper with tissue paper, washi tape, and scrapbook paper.

6. When it's time to party, distribute these, have everyone pull back on the balloon, and let the good times and the confetti fly.

SPRINKLE IN THE SPECIAL

Create a party favor station near the front door that has all the fixings for the homemade poppers ready to go so everyone can make and take a few home. Consider writing fun phrases on red, white, and blue tie tags. They add an extra sprinkle of spirit. Possible phrases:

YOU'RE A SPARK OF JOY!

LET FREEDOM RING!

YOU ARE STAR-SPANGLED SPECIAL.

SHINE ON!

Patriotic Punch

Go ahead, be courageous. Add brave, bold colors and flavors to the beverage table with this creative cocktail!

- 1 cup cranapple juice
- 1 cup piña colada mix
- 1 cup blue G2 Gatorade

Pour in the order you want the colors to layer, and garnish with a Twizzler or striped paper straw.

Star-Spangled Skewers

Skip the expensive fruit tray and set out these simple, sweet skewers!

- 1 watermelon, cut in half
- Blueberries
- Strawberries
- Raspberries
- Other fruits as desired
- Skewers

Cut the watermelon in half and spoon the fruit out of one side. Place the hulled side down on a tray. Arrange the fruits on skewers and stick them into the watermelon. This makes a fun display and simplifies the chore of serving!

Firecracker Marshmallows

Choose this sweet treat for a quick and simple snack that will set off even the littlest firecrackers!

- Bag of jumbo marshmallows
- White chocolate candy melts
- Blue food coloring
- Jar of cherries

Melt your white chocolate and add food coloring to the desired hue. Dip one side of a marshmallow into the blue chocolate and set chocolate side up onto wax paper. Dry a cherry with a paper towel, then add the cherry to the top of the marshmallow while the chocolate is melted so it attaches. Repeat. Allow the chocolate to fully set—and enjoy!

PJ Spa Night

Suggest a spa session and watch all your friends speed over to check out your salts and scrubs! Women juggle so many responsibilities and keep track of the needs of their family and their adopted family of neighbors, friends, and others. I'm sure you know several who could use an evening of self-care and sisterhood. Amen?

I'll guide you through ideas for refreshing snacks that are easy to handle even with wet nails or while lounging and chatting. You'll think you've died and gone to heaven with a divine treatment that takes minutes to prep yet offers a sense of indulgence. Give guests a true spa experience with at-home hacks like warm towels from your Crock-Pot. Simply amazing!

Your girls will be guessing the beauty brand of your secret scrub. Wait 'til you rock their socks with the recipe. Whether you're celebrating a specific occasion or hosting a Saturday night for your best gal pals, this spa night is sure to be a sensation.

PARTY POSSIBILITIES

This party theme would be perfect for a bridal shower or a low-key bachelorette party. Pamper your prettiest parent with a mature skin mask and moisturizer application for Mother's Day. What group of girls wouldn't squeal over a spa night slumber party? Not a fan of facials—make it all about the mani-pedi!

All Things Fresh and Floral!

Think about what you like best about the environment at your favorite spa. Consider how you can showcase those same scents and embellishments you adore. Feature similar flowers if you particularly enjoy the florals. Passionate about their particular soap pump? Pick up a similar dispenser, and fill it with one of your products or a sensational scented soap.

Organize and display all your pretty products in a pleasing way with a traveling tray. Rather than setting yourself up for a self-serve disaster, distribute single-use amounts of products onto a traveling tray for each of your guests.

tip Add a little lavish touch to your travel trays by using rose petals as little product pods! Looks fancy and is fabulously easy to do.

Set up your spa counter on a table with your trays, fresh flowers, and individual mirrors for each guest.

While it might seem easier to let each sister serve herself, it saves time and makes such a pretty product display when you distribute the items ahead of time! This also ensures that each guest gets the perfect proportion and doesn't over or under partake of the product.

tip It may sound silly, but sliced cucumbers are everything at a spa night. Use them on your eyes, as ingredients for the infused water, or as embellishments on your traveling trays.

At-Home Hot Towel

Who says decor is only about things you can see? Let the peace-giving scent of lavender create the spa experience in your home. This lovely extra touch takes only minutes and adds to the party's ambience while creating the luxurious heated towel experience for pamper-worthy pals.

1. Fill a Crock-Pot a little over halfway with water.

2. Roll the towels and set them in the water inside the Crock-Pot.

3. Set the Crock-Pot to low.

4. Drop in 2 to 3 lavender essential oil drops and put the lid on.

5. Let the towels warm for 30 minutes.

6. Test the temperature on your arm and have spare, dry towels available to catch any drips. The best part? Your home will be infused with the gentle essence of lavender and transport every guest to the happy place of a spa sanctuary.

Simple Sugar Scrub

Skip the expense of a brand name or fancy packaging and DIY this scrub with ingredients you probably already have at home!

ALL YOU'LL NEED: Epsom salts, brown sugar, coconut oil, lavender essential oil

1. Combine equal parts Epsom salts and brown sugar.

2. Add coconut oil to create a paste texture.

3. Add 1 to 2 drops of lavender essential oil.

4. Stir up and scrub away!

BRITTANY'S SPA DAY FAVORITES

1. Mirror

2. Cream cleanser

3. Moisturizing lotion

4. Face mask

5. Sugar scrub

6. Under-eye soother patch

7. Facial wipes

SPRINKLE IN THE SPECIAL

No need for friends to miss the bliss. Send them each home with a small bag containing a small portion of the homemade sugar scrub along with the recipe written on a piece of cardstock. Add a few of your favorite single-serve or travel-sized lotions. Include a written verse to refresh their spirit, such as: "I will refresh the weary" (Jeremiah 31:25).

Carry-Along Salad Cups

Nobody wants to do dishes on spa night, so serve your salad in travel-friendly tumblers!

- Kale or lettuce of choice
- Cranberries
- Broccoli slaw
- Dressing
- Chicken
- Sunflower seeds

Combine the salad ingredients in a large bowl and distribute them into plastic tumblers with a fork. Serve immediately or store dressing separately until served.

Portable PB&J Kabobs

Stick with the sans serveware goal and pass around these convenient kabobs. Their convenience starts for you and your prep and continues during the party as your guests can eat and be pampered with ease.

- Peanut butter
- Jelly
- Bread
- Bananas
- Strawberries
- Blueberries
- Raspberries
- Other favorite fruit choices

Prepare and slice PB&J sandwiches into small squares. Layer those with sliced fruit onto kabob sticks and serve with a smile.

Infused Water

These libations look lavish! Spoil guests and serve in cute single serve bottles.

- Cucumbers
- Watermelon
- Mint sprigs
- Strawberries

- Lime slices
- Lemon slices
- Orange slices

Slice the ingredients small enough to fit through the lip of the glass bottles. Add the desired ingredients to the bottles and then fill with water and ice.

Backyard Movie Night

Bring the best features of the cinema to your own backyard. Invite your focus group of friends over for an outdoor movie night. They'll sit back and enjoy nature's overhead projection of stars while you project a favorite flick onto a big screen.

Nothing but the best for your audience. Invite them to snack on all the same goodies that you'd get at the theater, plus all the popcorn they can put away. When you combine treats with the sweet comforts of home, it makes for a spectacular summer celebration your family and friends will savor.

Serve up halfway-homemade bites that even your toughest critics will give rave reviews. During intermission, guests can take five on the pillow pads your production manager pieced together. Be sure to credit the special effects crew when everyone is complimenting your popcorn petals centerpieces.

This evening is casual and enjoyable. So much so that you'll want to plan a sequel right away.

PARTY POSSIBILITIES

I think any evening of the week is an excuse to host this box-office winning gathering. It's also a versatile theme that can shine the spotlight on any special day or person. Celebrate a movie buff. Reward a child for finishing a project by hosting this as a slumber party. Or turn up the glam and host a gal gala. Invite friends to dress up and bring a favorite appetizer to pass around.

Starring Role Decor

Put this party together on the patio. Whether you use a regular projector and screen or take the TV outside, you'll make this an affair to remember. Warm up the concrete by bringing out an area rug from one of your interior rooms. Increase the cozy factor with lots of layered blankets and throw pillows. I have a few ideas for you to make this the special edition movie night. It's the director's cut of backyard parties.

Fan out some full-sized chocolate bars and boxes of movie candy as edible decor to create an at-home concession stand. I'm not the only one with this fantasy, right? Pick up a roll of tickets, and you'll get lots of decor mileage out of them. Hang them like a garland, tear off a long strand and stick it in a clear jar, or keep the roll together and use it as a base for a serving plate or for your popcorn petals centerpiece.

If you want to get a thumbs-up for your cinema beverage options, set up a root beer float bar! Fill up a large tub with ice. Tuck glasses, root beer bottles, and a plastic container of ice cream down into the ice to chill. Set out some cute straws, an ice-cream scoop—and don't forget the sundae fixin's. (Helloooo, sprinkles!)

Have so many guests that you need a furniture stunt double? No problem. Turn a regular storage crate into a snack table, foot rest, or additional seating for the show. Pop a pillow on top for additional seating if the neighbors drop by! Cover a crib mattress with a fitted sheet, or even use a trusty travel blow-up. Like the storage crates, pillow poufs can also double as seats and tables.

tip Snacks organized on trays are easily passed around so guests don't have to get up during the film. Or if you have a child who loves to work the crowd, have them serve snacks up and down the aisles.

And storage squares can be flipped around to make a great table for guests seated lower to the ground who don't want to get up and head to a buffet line during the show.

Film reels make an IMAX impact. If you don't have any, ask your church or school if they have any you could borrow for the event.

Snuggle Station

Stretching out on the patio is plenty comfy with this DIY pillow pad. This is so easy, you might want to make one in a special fabric for each season.

ALL YOU'LL NEED: two yards fabric, three 20 x 26-inch pillows, and your favorite method of sewing

1. Fold the two yards of fabric in half the long way.

2. Turn it inside out and sew the ends together.

3. Turn it right side out.

4. Put one of the pillows on top of the fabric and mark where your next seam will be.

5. Sew a straight stitch for that section and then one more time for the last pillow.

6. You'll have three sections to insert your pillows.

7. Leave the edge open to remove or replace the pillows for easy washing.

Academy Voting Night

Create your own on-the-spot award night. Have ballots written up and printed and a set of pens ready. Get your movie-house crowd's expert opinions. Invite each guest to vote on:

- Best actor/actress

- Best supporting actor/actress

- Best scene

- Worst scene

- Best nonspeaking role

- Best animal role

You can make the list long and silly or ask your resident warm-up act to invent the categories. When the movie is over, collect and tally the votes and share the results. If there is a tie, welcome critics to stand up and state the case for their vote.

A Poppin' Centerpiece

Has a simple floral arrangement ever looked so...appetizing? That's right. These cinema-inspired centerpieces really set the scene for movie night.

ALL YOU'LL NEED: a bouquet of white and yellow flowers, popcorn boxes from a craft store or the grocery store

1. Cut the flower stem ends at an angle to create varied lengths.

2. Choose a base length that allows the blooms to rest at the top of the box.

3. Intermix white and yellow flowers so the blooms resemble puffs of popcorn.

4. Assemble the arrangement and place it where your moviegoers can gawk!

5. If you want the flowers to last for a second showing, place a jar with water in the popcorn box before adding the stems. They will inspire joy for days.

Reel Brownie Dip

All the brownie flavor you love without the bummer of baking!

- 1 (8 oz.) package cream cheese, softened
- 1 (8 oz.) container whipped topping
- 1 (18 oz.) box brownie mix, dry
- 2 T. milk
- 1 cup mini chocolate chips
- Strawberries or graham crackers for dipping

In a large mixing bowl, beat the cream cheese until smooth. Add the whipped topping and stir until smooth. Blend in the brownie mix and the milk. Mix until smooth. Fold in the chocolate chips and serve.

Showtime Pretzel Bites

These taste even better than those at the cinema! Dip these bits into zesty honey mustard and enjoy the show.

- 1 tube or container of premade pizza dough
- ⅓ cup baking soda
- 1 egg, beaten

Preheat the oven to 425°. Roll out the pizza dough onto a pan or cutting board. Cut the dough into 2-inch squares and then roll it into balls.

In a deep pot, bring 2 quarts of water to a boil. Toss in the baking soda and stir.

Add the dough balls and cook for 2 minutes, and then remove them with a slotted spoon and place them on a cookie sheet covered in parchment paper. Brush the dough balls with egg and sprinkle with salt. Bake until golden brown (about 15 minutes).

Turkey and Dill Pinwheels

Pass a plate of these pinwheels around the patio during the previews!

- 8 tortilla wraps
- 1 (8 oz.) package cream cheese, softened
- 2 T. fresh dill, chopped
- 1 to 2 tsp. onion salt
- 1 (8 oz.) package turkey slices

Mix the cream cheese, dill, and salt. Spread onto the tortilla wraps. Add the turkey slices. Roll up and slice into pinwheels.

FAMILY FRIENDLY MOVIES

THE SANDLOT	DR. DOOLITTLE
TOY STORY	HOMEWARD BOUND
LITTLE RASCALS	EVAN ALMIGHTY
JUMANJI	BEETHOVEN
MRS. DOUBTFIRE	CHARLOTTE'S WEB
FREAKY FRIDAY	HOOK
LITTLE GIANTS	HONEY I SHRUNK THE KIDS

Back to School CELEBRATION

Fall offers up so many beginnings to capture in one's heart and photo albums. Going back to school is a golden opportunity to create awesome memories as you kick off the learning season with creativity and a smile.

Put a positive spin on study sessions with snacks kids will love. Set your scholars up for success by creating a strategic station for school supplies and homework organization. And snap those pics when you can because your child's personality and style will shine through each time you look at those images in the years ahead.

The colorful pages ahead are your parent packet—all you need to know to make smarty-pants snacks, class-y crafts, and school days decor. Go to the head of the class and host a party for your family, friends, and neighborhood kids and parents. Your decorations and the homework station will inspire your guests to honor learning in their own way at home.

PARTY POSSIBILITIES

These ideas aren't only for the first days of classes. Break them out to celebrate special occasions throughout the school year: a positive note home, good grades, behavior improvement, showing citizenship and leadership skills. When we look for them, these opportunities arise often.

Decorate to Educate

Let's face it, your kids are likely to be more into the snacks than the way you style your home. However, each time you add a decoration feature that salutes their school experience, you reinforce the importance of education. Your creative efforts will inspire their creativity to flourish. Mama, nothing is wasted. Don't ever forget that.

A clever double vase featuring fun alphabet magnets celebrates the building blocks of language. Place a small, clear jar or vase inside a slightly larger clear glass container. Fill the space between with colorful alphabet magnets. Add some fresh-cut flowers or grocery-store stems to the center. Consider having plants with scents that stimulate memory and the senses, like rosemary or peppermint.

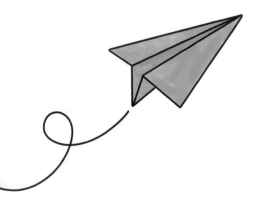

Use old cards for a charming vintage vibe or new cards with bright, expressive colors to create a banner worthy of top marks. Choose a twine or decorative strand that complements your card style. Clip the cards to the twine with cute clothespins and hang as desired.

tip All the creative crafts make wonderful gifts for teachers, tutors, and other helpers during the year. Do you have a go-to, champion carpool driver? Celebrate him or her.

tip Create a portable homework station. Even if you have a homework headquarters, an easy-travel kit is handy for afternoons at the home of a neighbor or grandparent.

Succulents Rule!

Other vases can't measure up to this succulent with a school-supply spin. Have this craft set up for the moms and kids to create together.

ALL YOU'LL NEED: vases or jars, rulers cut in pieces to measure slightly higher than the vessels, hot glue gun, plants

Have each parent-child team:

1. Select a small glass jar or vase.

2. Choose pieces of rulers to suit their vase's height. (Have parents do any cutting.)

3. Line up the ruler pieces, numbers facing out, and hot glue to the vase.

4. Set the succulent with filler inside.

5. If you're aiming for the head of the class, add an apple embellishment cut from cardstock or construction paper and attach it with a small clothespin.

PENCILS AND PENS

ERASERS

PAPER AND NOTEPADS

MARKERS

RULER

GLUE STICK

SCISSORS

PAPER CLIPS

STICKY NOTES
IN FAVORITE COLORS

DATE PLANNER

INSPIRATIONAL STICKERS

If your kiddos don't yet have homework, set up this area as a creation station or imagination station (like a craft stash for kids!). Include tape, ribbons, markers, and sketch paper.

Homework Headquarters

A homework station is a strategic, inspiring way to help your kids enjoy learning. This simple DIY for your home organizes a space to hold all the necessary supplies. Just think—no more stalling productivity by running all over the house looking for missing papers.

1. Choose a spot in your home, such as the corner of a room, a closet (or the bottom half of one), or a desk.

2. Clear the space to start with a clean slate.

3. Add small jars and containers.

4. Fill the containers with grade-relevant supplies.

5. Sprinkle in inspiring colors, photos, or quotes.

6. If there is a wall, hang up a calendar, chalkboard, or corkboard.

I like the openness of our homework station. The instant accessibility to the supplies is motivating. Invite your kid to participate in choosing the elements that make the space bright and inviting. They can focus on the fun while you focus on the function.

SPRINKLE IN THE SPECIAL

While the DIY helps your littles at home, take the opportunity to share a small basket of the same supplies with guests at your party. Let each child decorate a tray, box, or basket with glitter, pom-poms, drawings, and streamers. Choose containers with lids or closures, and fill them with basic supplies. It's nice to have a bit of home on the go, even when it's related to homework.

YUM!

A+ Apple Sandwiches

From sack lunch to snack time, these apple sandwiches score high on the taste test.

- Apples
- Peanut butter
- Cereal

Remove the cores from the apples and cut into ¼- to ½-inch slices. Spread each slice with peanut butter. Top with your favorite cereal.

Berry-Smart Whips

These adorable strawberry stacks come together so quick and easy. Whip them up for those impromptu study sessions. They are as simple as:

1. Place a dollop of whipped cream onto a cracker.

2. Top with a strawberry slice.

3. Enjoy the crunch, the cream, and the sweet burst of berry.

Write Stuff Cookies

Whether your kiddos are learning their alphabet or composing essays, they'll have the write stuff with these wafer pencil cookies.

- Vanilla sugar wafer cookies
- White candy melts
- Red food coloring
- Mini chocolate chips

Prepare white candy melts and add a few drops of red food coloring to create the desired shade of eraser pink. When ready, dab some of this mixture onto one end of each wafer cookie. Use a sharp knife to gently cut the shape of a point on the other end of each. For the finishing touch, press a perfect mini chocolate chip into just a touch of candy melts on the point for the tip of the pencil.

Champion Tailgater Gathering

Pull up to the game like a pro on the go. Get your squad pumped up with finger food fixin's to fuel them through all four quarters. Your touchdown decor will have the opponent calling for a replay to figure out how you pulled it off! (They will be taking notes.) Customize details with your team colors and with mascots or logos if you are going the extra yard. Each craft and menu item is an easy tackle that will come together in a snap.

Three cheers for flexibility! You don't have to arrive hours early to a game or be camped in a stadium parking lot to experience the casual fun and fellowship of tailgating. Park the party in the backyard or gather up the gang in the garage. It's about the vibe, not the vehicle. I am here to cheer you on through this winning party. The steps are simple, and the planning, setup, and cleanup won't send you into overtime.

Enjoy your time. No ref is going to blow the whistle if everything isn't perfect. No rules, no fouls, no penalties! Just like die-hard fans, your friends and family will still be all cheers even if you have a couple fumbles. With these tips and tricks, I'm betting that you'll be voted best home team manager of the season.

PARTY POSSIBILITIES

The occasion to use this is open for a coin flip! Here are a few that might make the cut: gathering to watch the big game on TV, celebrating a travel-team win, wrapping up a Little League season, or honoring the birthday of an avid sports fan.

Indoor-Outdoor Decor

Drop the tailgate, raise the back hatch, or clear your dining table and drape it with a team throw as a fan-worthy tablecloth. As you plan for any of the decor ideas or crafts, shop your home first. If your team color is red, bust out that red-and-white-striped pillow you include in your Valentine's Day accessory stash. Being budget-conscious helps us become more creative celebrators.

Mix black-and-white patterns with pops of team colors. Toss in neutrals to balance or calm a color craze. Don't be afraid to feature flowers in your finishing touches.

 tip Score a winning pass! From your kitchen or tailgater, send a tray of food into the crowd to be shared. No buffet line or serving surface area is needed!

Bold Banner

Make it a banner year and a banner party. Create these cute, retro banners in advance for decor statement pieces, or have the supplies available for others to create their own.

ALL YOU'LL NEED: a banner kit or cardstock in desired colors, twine/ribbon, green marker, paper hole punch if needed

1. Add letters to your banner.

2. If holes are needed, use a paper hole punch or sharp knife.

3. Add squiggles with a green paint marker to look like grass.

4. Use twine or ribbon ties to secure your banner pieces in order.

5. Time to cheer. This is rookie friendly with first-string results.

I picked a coordinating buffalo plaid set of letter stickers to complement the pattern of the ribbon on the banner. My banner kit came with brown craft paper, so we cut white strips from regular copy paper and pasted them on the football seams.

Classic Pennant

Give your crowd a clever craft for halftime entertainment. You can create a couple of these spirited pennants in advance for your party's decor, and then give guests, young and old, a play-by-play to create their own.

ALL YOU'LL NEED: precut pennants or cardstock, hot glue gun, no-sew letters from the fabric department, ribbon, kabob sticks

1. Select the precut pennant of choice or cut cardstock into a pennant shape.

2. With hot glue, affix sporty no-sew letters or those cut from cardstock.

3. Trim the pennants with ribbon for added color and flash.

4. Tape or glue the wide end of the pennant to a kabob stick.

Place the finished pennants in a planter or vase for a fun centerpiece or sideline touch. Or pin pennants to the wall or a corkboard for backdrop cheer. If guests make their own, get a trading-card-worthy photo of them with their creation.

SPRINKLE IN THE SPECIAL

Give the biggest fan a fantastic surprise. Create a banner or pennant with sparkles and a personal touch. Use a glitter pen to add the individual's name alongside #1 Fan.

Centerpiece in a Snap

Bring some trendy team spirit to your tailgate setup or dining space by featuring fresh florals in the starting lineup. It's an unexpected move sure to turn sports fanatics into fans of clever decor.

ALL YOU'LL NEED: jar, football you can cut, fresh flowers (consider team colors) or faux ones

1. Grab your sacrificial football. (Make die-hard footballers look away for the next part.)

2. Create a starter cut on both ends of ball with a sharp knife. Use the white line as the guide.

3. With scissors, finish cutting off both ends of the football.

4. Slide the football over your jar. You may need to cut a short slit along the side of the ball for it to fit.

5. Add water and fresh flowers or your faux flowers.

TOUCHDOWN!

Burger Bites

If your team is in the mood for burgers but the weather is too moody to bust out the grill, never fear. Bring the party inside and bake some burger bites. Easy to make, easy to eat, and easy to love. These bites are not only incredibly delicious, but also a low carb, healthy, FUN meal to prepare and enjoy!

- Ground beef
- Your favorite burger fixin's: tomato, lettuce, pickle, cheese, mayonnaise, etc.
- Toothpicks

Preheat the oven to 400°.

Season your ground beef as you would for grilled burgers and roll it into bite-sized meatballs.

Bake for 20 minutes or until cooked through. Slide a toothpick through the burger bite and top it with your usual favorites!

tip
If you use lean beef, you will have less drippings.

Touchdown Dip

Peanut butter goes head to head with cream cheese as vanilla wafers and sliced fruit cheer from the sideline. This dip scores big!

- 1 (8 oz.) package cream cheese, softened
- 1 cup smooth peanut butter
- 1 (8 oz.) container whipped cream, divided
- 1 cup beer nuts (or honey-roasted peanuts)
- ½ cup chocolate sprinkles
- Vanilla wafers
- Sliced fruit such as apples

Combine the cream cheese and peanut butter in a large bowl; mix thoroughly. Save ¼ cup of the whipped cream in a resealable plastic bag and place it in the freezer. Fold half of the remaining whipped cream into the dip mixture. Once fully mixed, fold in the other half along with the beer nuts until fully combined.

Place a large sheet of plastic wrap on a flat surface. Scoop the dip out of the bowl and onto the center of the plastic wrap in an oval. Wrap the dip completely in the plastic, and pat it into the shape of a football. Set the ball on a plate and place it in the freezer for 60 to 90 minutes. You want the ball to be solid but still soft enough to dip into.

Unwrap the ball and coat the top and sides with chocolate sprinkles. Take the bag of reserved whipped cream out of the freezer and cut a small hole in one corner to create a piping bag. Pipe white laces on top of the football dip. Finally, place your creation in the center of a serving plate and fill the sides with vanilla wafers and sliced fruit for dipping. Allow the dip to soften for about 20 minutes and then stand back and watch the huddle form.

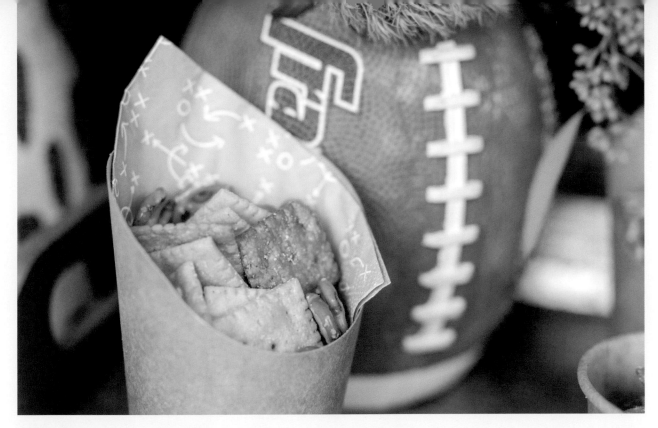

Championship Combo Mix

This lineup of ingredients teams up with a squad of seasonings that are sure to bring home the win.

- 6 cups rice cereal (like Rice Chex)
- 2 cups mixed nuts
- 5 cups pretzels
- 2 cups cheese crackers
- 2 cups oyster crackers
- 1 cup sesame sticks

- 6 T. unsalted butter, melted
- 2 (.07 oz.) packets Italian seasoning salad dressing dry powder mix
- 2 tsp. ranch seasoning dry mix
- 2 tsp. mustard powder
- ½ cup grated Parmesan cheese
- 1 T. dried parsley flakes

Preheat the oven to 300°.

In an extra-large mixing bowl, combine the rice cereal, nuts, pretzels, cheese crackers, oyster crackers, and sesame sticks and gently toss/stir. Melt the butter and stir it into the mixture in the bowl. Combine the Italian seasoning, ranch seasoning mix, mustard powder, Parmesan cheese, and parsley flakes. Save one tablespoon of the mixture as a final garnish; set aside. Sprinkle the remaining seasoning combo over the top of the cereal/cracker mixture, then carefully stir everything together. Pour the mixture evenly over a large cookie sheet.

Bake in the oven for 30 minutes, stirring the contents halfway through the baking time. When cooked, sprinkle the saved tablespoon of seasoning on the top. Add the extra grated Parmesan cheese and dried parsley if desired. Allow the mixture to cool and then store it in an airtight container. Serve at room temperature.

Eat, Drink & Be Spooky

Gather up your ghouls and goblins for this howling Halloween party. Guests will be calling you the ghostess with the mostest when they're tempted by the tasty treats and cryptic crafts.

I'm more into cute than creepy, so I'm sharing a sweetly spooky style that is a crowd-pleaser whether you're hosting adults or a mix of mummies and littles. No magic is required to dress up a few desserts, your table display, and some dollar store buckets.

If you want to focus on celebrating the harvest season, there are several "just right without the fright" offerings. Whichever way you like to celebrate All Hallows' Eve, consider hosting this as a costume party. Before the night is through, vote on the most creative or creepy creation!

It's all about bringing people together. Believe me... they'll love the treats, and you'll love these tricks to a successful, easy party.

PARTY POSSIBILITIES

If you dare to scare on a non-Halloween night, break out this thrilling theme for any Friday the thirteenth or to host a full-moon scary movie night. The kiddos might be enticed by a *Hocus-Pocus* or *Monster High* party. The season premiere or finale of *Stranger Things* would bring all the teens together.

Never Fear the Unexpected

Don't be afraid to spark ingenuity with colors beyond traditional schemes. I highlighted the expected orange with splashes of black and white in patterns of stripes and dots. Adding pink to my palette opened the way for inclusion of decor and craft pieces from previous parties!

Papier-mâché or plastic pumpkins in bright colors can be reused from year to year and even occasion to occasion for gourd-geous centerpieces.

tip After the guests have arrived, move your grisly gaze door decor inside for the party and surround it with black bats for a fang-tastic focus wall. Or make two!

SPRINKLE IN THE SPECIAL

Pssst. Spray paint is your pal when you can't find the item you want in the color you need! This expands your color palette and your budget because when all you find (on the cheap) is basic orange, you know what to do.

I love using a bar cart! It allows for simple setup and is a lifesaver when you need more counter surfaces or serving areas. Every busy hostess is thankful for flexible choices. A bar cart can be rolled room to room or out to the patio or deck.

If you are a gal who prefers the creepy factor over the cute, feel free to lose the bows and ribbons and bring in the webs and skulls and serve up a more gruesome line of goodies such as gummi spiders and worms. If you host an adults-only event, you can serve an elusive elixir from the bar cart to go along with your theme.

tip Use multiple bar carts to create snack and beverage stations in different areas of the room, home, or yard. You expand the mileage for your decor and resolve the dreaded food table traffic jam.

Feather Me Spooky Wreath

All eyes will be on this dreadfully delightful door decor. Pick up a feathered wreath at your local craft store or wrap a feather boa around a regular wreath for a similar effect. Glue googly eyes in a variety of sizes around the wreath for an eye-deal addition.

tip

Pretty has its place at a party, and so does pretty unexpected—like an upside-down character. I filled a huge pumpkin with stuffing and paper shreds and then added crazy leg picks and plastic spiders for a topsy-turvy tablescape addition. If you like slightly spooky more than all-out silly, use skeleton legs.

Buckets and Ballots

Give your dollar store buckets a makeover! I created these as party favors, but you can turn this into a super fun group DIY, so every guest can create a costume competition ballot box.

1. First, remove the plastic handle of each dollar store bucket.

2. Have a variety of ribbon options.

3. Twist some ribbon tightly and feed it through the handle hole from outside to inside.

4. Feed your ribbon from the outside in through the other handle hole.

5. Determine the length of handle you want, then tie each side in a quick, tight knot.

6. Trim the excess.

7. Using the same ribbon (or introduce a new color if you want), tie a bow around each side where the ribbon meets the bucket.

8. Let the voting begin. These make great ghostly gifts, devilishly darling decor pieces, party favor to-go containers, and trick-or-treat goodie buckets.

Mummy's Brownies

Keep their sweet tooth under wraps with this sweet treat.

- 1 box brownie mix
- White icing
- Candy eyes

Prepare the brownies as directed. Use a circle cookie cutter to cut the brownies into round bites. Drizzle white icing over the top and add the candy eyes. That's a wrap!

Costume Competition

Host a friendly competition. Invite guests to dress up to suit whichever theme you go for:

Movie or book characters

People from history

Monsters and Halloween ghouls

Frankenstein (or another celebrity creature) look-alike

Set categories for the votes:

- most creative
- best use of found-at-home materials
- most ghoulish
- most colorful
- best look-alike

Create the ballot slips and instruct the guests to cast their votes throughout the party. Who needs a ballot box? Follow the DIY steps for the Buckets and Ballots, and you're set.

All Eyes on the Creepy Cake

Eye spy a halfway-homemade dessert that's a scream!

- Store-bought cake
- Cotton candy
- Candy eyes
- Plastic spiders

Cover the grocery store cake in cotton candy. Decorate it with candy eyes and plastic spiders. Serve up a scream!

Pepper Pumpkin Stack

Slightly more sophisticated spine-chill seekers will be thrilled to sink their fangs into one of these stacks when hunger pangs hit.

- Snack crackers
- Brie
- Pepper jelly
- Rosemary sprigs

Place a slice of Brie on a snack cracker and top it with a spoonful of pepper jelly. Add a sprig of rosemary to complete your pepper pumpkin stack.

Cupcakes & Crafts

"Party please...with sugar on top?" Has anyone in your circle of friends been begging for a get-together of tasty wonders? If so, immediately set a date on your event calendar to host this gathering. If not, then immediately set that date anyway! And lead the way to a frosted frontier where any sugar-seeking sister will find her bliss.

Treats and sweets serve up inspiration for clever crafts. It is entertainment at its yummy best. Let the conversation and sugar-induced celebration unfold. Whether you're honoring a sixth or sixtieth birthday or hosting a just-because "life is sweet" themed afternoon, the fixin's on these pages offer the perfect combination of engaging activities and delectable indulgences.

To top off the cupcake extravaganza, there is a DIY that your guests will be delighted to make and take with them.

PARTY POSSIBILITIES

Planning a wedding or baby shower for a friend? Simply choose a color scheme that coordinates and let the cupcakes bake. A young girl's birthday party becomes a time of crafting poms to use in her room decor. Invite each of her friends to make pom-poms for themselves and a couple for the guest of honor to string together as a garland to drape over a closet door-way or a bed's canopy. Wait a second...I would want that too!

Before a big sports season begins, have some friends over to create poms in the colors of a favorite school or pro team. Everyone gets to go home with a palm pom...think of it as a worry stone when a game gets really intense.

Pretty Is Baked In

The showstopping desserts and extra dollops of decor delight
turn a Sunday afternoon into a special day of joy, creating, and
connecting. Your guests will be smiling the moment they feast
their eyes on your fun-flowing table and special touches.

Cupcake liners belong in kitchens *and* craft closets. Who knew? Grab a supply of multicolored liners and a needle and yarn. Flatten the liners and then use your yarn or twine to string to them together from top to top and bottom to bottom. It's that simple.

I chose to adorn this party with colors that speak to my friends and me— colors we love to wear and bring into our homes. I included Certified Celebrator theme items as well, like pom-poms and tassels. Customize your event with the extras your family and friends are partial to: greenery, florals, wreaths, lights, etc.

tip If you would rather not supply all the materials, ask friends to bring their own supplies, or have each person bring one craft supply to share with the group.

Precious Pom-Pom Letter

I absolutely adore these pom-poms. They can be used many wonderful ways. For this gathering, I invited my friends to glue poms to a wooden initial. Introduce your group to the power of the pom.

ALL YOU'LL NEED: skeins of yarn in a variety of colors to please your peeps

1. Place the end of the yarn on your fingers. (We used four fingers for larger poms.)

2. Wrap the yarn around your fingers (not too tight).

3. Keep wrapping until you reach the desired fullness.

4. Cut the thread trail.

5. Measure and cut an additional piece of yarn long enough to tie around the pom-pom in process and have some excess.

6. Insert the end of the yarn between your fingers and pull it through the other side.

7. The piece of yarn is now on one side of the pom-pom.

8. Wrap the yarn strand through the fingertips, and tie the beginning of a knot. Pull tight.

9. Carefully slide the yarn off your fingers.

10. Pull the yarn tight and finish the knot.

11. Slide your scissors into the loops and cut all the way around the pom-pom.

12. Keep your long pieces out of the way. Trim any pieces as desired.

tip
Hot glue a pom-pom to a magnet or thread through a paperclip for added flare that would make a darling little gift.

THE CRAFT MENU

At the heart of this party is the craft menu. It inspires guests to try something new that helps them express their creativity.

SPRINKLE IN THE SPECIAL

Gather up your church group gals or prayer circle sisters for an evening event together. You'll craft and pray your way through a batch of prayer poms. After your time of prayer for those on your heart, attach a small verse or prayer to a pom that you'll give to the intended recipient. Get your kids involved in the fun.

Whimsical Wood Bead Necklaces

This craft inspires guests to express their true creative colors and wear them with pride.

ALL YOU'LL NEED: wood beads of various sizes from the jewelry section of the craft store, acrylic paints in various colors, kabob sticks, leather strands in lengths for bracelets or necklaces

1. Thread a couple beads on a kabob stick.

2. Use the stick as a handle while painting the beads.

3. Let the beads dry.

4. Thread painted, personalized beads onto a leather strand.

5. Finish with a secure knot so it can be slipped over the wrist or head.

TO CREATE A CLASP:

1. Keep the ends separate.

2. Secure a painted bead at one end of the leather strap with a knot.

3. On the other end, form a loop about the size of the anchor bead. Voilà!

This project is not just for kids. My adult friends enjoyed it and loved the end products. They wanted to keep making them.

Pepperoni Puffs

This fun-sized Italian dish is a pizza cake to put together.

- Refrigerated pizza crust
- Pizza sauce
- Mozzarella cheese
- Pepperoni
- Other favorite pizza toppings

Preheat the oven to 350°.

Layer the ingredients on the pizza crust and bake for 25 minutes or until the pizza is completely cooked.

Pink Lemonade Cupcake

Save time with this halfway-homemade spin on this flavor favorite.

Strawberry grocery-store cupcakes

Small wedges of lemon

Mint pieces

Simply top the grocery-store cupcakes with lemon wedges and sprigs of mint for a delicious, decorative finish.

Cup-Quake Shake

This concoction is off the scale when it comes to satisfying anyone's sweet tooth.

- Corn syrup
- Sprinkles
- Vanilla ice cream
- 1 cupcake
- Milk

Pour the corn syrup into a small bowl and use a brush to thinly coat the inside of a clear glass with the syrup. Pour the rainbow sprinkles into the glass. They will immediately stick to the corn syrup. Spread a little around the rim as well. Dip the rim into a shallow plate of sprinkles. Set aside.

Using a blender, mix the vanilla ice cream, one cupcake, and milk. The amount of milk used controls the frothiness of the shake. Pour the milkshake into your sprinkled glass. Now for the mind-blowing addition. Place a kabob stick in each glass and then thread and stack extra cupcakes on the skewer. This is literally an over-the-top sugar fix.

Chili Cook-off

Hungry for some friendly competition or the casual joy of an outdoor get-together? Satisfy these cravings with a chili cook-off! This is a favorite for many because your main event is all about showcasing (and judging) the meal. At the end of the activity, you and your guests get the delight of a yummy, hearty dish and the camaraderie of a contest. You choose the teams...will it be a family cook-off or neighbor takes on neighbor? Or will you take your culinary cues from the top cooking shows by hosting a kid version as well? I'll bet there is at least one future soup chef ready to be discovered in your crowd.

If you've been hosting indoor parties for a while, you'll wonder why you haven't *bean* cooking outdoors all along! Finishing touches to the festivities are equally breezy with simple outdoor decorations and a side of amazing cornbread (which will convince everyone to never hold a down-home cornbread competition if you're in the running). You're set. Grab an apron and jump into the cook-off.

PARTY POSSIBILITIES

A chili cook-off is great for a block party, a tailgate party, or a welcome-to-the-neighborhood meet and greet. Or host a soup-er bowl at work. Each participant signs up for a day of the week to bring their soup to school. Everyone tastes each soup and then, when everyone has had a day to share, you ask for votes. Lunch is covered for a week.

Prize Decor

Anytime a contest is involved, I love to use the prizes as part of the setting's visual adornments. What better way to stir up motivation and a competitive spirit, am I right? So, set up spoon prizes where all the participants can see. Your DIY Spoon of Success underscores the theme whether you place it on a wall or on the picnic table centerpiece. We'll walk through the instructions for all of these clever elements.

As you'll see, I keep all the other pieces "picnic simple."

I admit I have a thing for clean, crisp, white dishes. So even when serving something as casual as chili, I enjoy laying out a small spread of chili toppings in my snow-white set of serveware. There is so much versatility using what you have. Just add a few thematic pieces or decorations and roll with it!

Petite Prizes

Your contest participants will win big with these tiny tags that are easy to make. Find these tiny tags and spoons in the scrapbook section at your local craft store. Hot glue the spoons to the wooden tags. If you want to mark the first-, second-, and third-place winners, just use a paint marker to identify those numbers on the flip side. You could also write in categories, such as hottest, tastiest, most original, etc.

 tip Have guests bring their metal offerings for the craft. If they used canned beans or chiles, you'll have a perfect variety to recycle into fabulous desert-themed decor.

tip Whether you take it to your yard, patio, porch, or an area park, plan ahead for the heating sources to keep the chili offerings safe for all. Scout out the outlets so you have enough power for Crock-Pots, hot plates, or whatever your competitors are using to deliver the chili heat.

Desert Decor Centerpiece Craft

Give ordinary cans a snazzy touch of the Southwest. When guests aren't voting for a chili champ or dipping their cornbread, they'll gladly make this craft to add more to the decor and then take home as a parting gift.

ALL YOU'LL NEED: rinsed empty cans, variety of succulents, potting soil, ribbon

1. Check the can rims, smoothing down rough edges with pliers.

2. Fill the cans ⅓ to ½ full of potting soil.

3. Gently remove the succulents from their pots or garden packs.

4. Loosen the soil around the roots.

5. Set the succulents into the cans and add soil to fill.

6. Add a little fancy frill of ribbon around the rim to take the tin cans up a notch.

Spoon of Success

A do-in-advance DIY that can be displayed as decor, handed over as a hostess gift, or utilized as a prize if you decide you need a grand trophy.

ALL YOU'LL NEED: large decorative spoon, a frame with cardboard backing, scrapbook paper, hot glue gun

1. Cut the scrapbook paper to fit the frame.

2. Hot glue the paper to the cardboard backing.

3. Center the spoon within the frame and on the paper.

4. Glue the spoon down and let it dry.

Every-Tasty-Vote-Counts Competition

If you are hard core about this contest and want to keep the cook of each chili a secret until the winner is announced, there are a couple ways to achieve this. When labeling the pots, use a number instead of a recipe title or the cook's name.

Take it a step further by keeping all the soups in the kitchen and the guests in a different room. Have one nonvoting friend divvy out a taste for each person in small cups from every numbered entry. Ask for votes, and then announce the winner midway through the event.

Another possibility for this activity is to host a family version where the family creates the chili and brings it to a neighborhood gathering, a block party, or a multifamily party at the park. Invite neighbors, strangers passing by, and anyone else to sample the chilis and cast their vote. This becomes a very enjoyable way to connect people and share a meal.

SPRINKLE IN THE SPECIAL

If you plan to go BIG and host an event at the park or other public area, elevate the competition. Invite a local chef, food writer, food blogger, or online restaurant reviewer to be the final judge of a cook-off or to announce the winner after everyone has voted.

Championship Chili

No need to research rare recipes. Keep it classic for the win!

- 1 (1.25 oz.) package chili seasoning mix
- 1 (15 oz.) can kidney beans, drained
- 1 (15 oz.) can chili beans, drained
- 1 (46 oz.) can tomato juice
- 1 (14.5 oz.) can diced tomatoes
- 1 lb. ground beef

Combine all the ingredients in a large pot. Stir and simmer for about 2 hours and allow to cool. Reheat on the stovetop and serve.

Winning White Chicken Chili

Take this competition a little south of the border with green chiles and a hint of lime!

- Rotisserie chicken
- 1 (15 oz.) can great northern beans, drained
- 1 (4.5 oz) can chopped green chiles
- 1 (32 oz.) box chicken broth
- Cilantro, set aside
- 1 lime, set aside

Combine all the ingredients, minus the cilantro and lime. Stir and simmer approximately 2 hours. Garnish with cilantro and a squeeze of lime before serving.

No-Contest Cornbread

Move over crackers—chili has a new companion!

- 1 (8.5 oz.) box Jiffy cornbread mix
- ½ (4.5 oz.) can green chiles
- ½ cup shredded cheddar cheese
- ½ cup sour cream
- ¼ cup milk
- 1 egg

Preheat the oven to 400°.

Combine the ingredients and stir to the consistency of pudding. Prepare a muffin pan with nonstick spray. Pour the mix into the muffin cups and bake for 15 to 20 minutes.

Pilgrim Party

Hosting for the holidays can intimidate the best of us because we think a gathering has to be perfect. Don't believe it, Mama. If you've ever held back your creativity while hosting or held back from hosting altogether, then let's celebrate this Thanksgiving without that hang-up, the hassle, or the humdrum-stick. You'll become the hostess you've always wanted to be as you serve up creativity to honor the best tradition—gathering together.

Lots of people share a holiday meal with more than one group: immediate family, the in-laws, longtime friends, church groups. In one weekend or even a 24-hour period, a person can dine on the same foods over and again. That's not all bad. Can anyone ever have enough sweet potatoes with brown sugar? However, if you're ready to host a harvest of fresh food traditions, I propose this gathering that's as easy as pumpkin pie to put together.

It's a new world, pilgrim! So break out your charcuterie board and express gratitude for life, blessings, and the people you gather in a new way.

PARTY POSSIBILITIES

I'm thankful that thankfulness can be celebrated year-round. So, choose an ordinary day and anoint it as an attitude of gratitude gathering. Maybe you want to thank people who have been helpful to you and your family.

All the Fabulous Trimmings

I turned to food options as a strong element in the decor. You can achieve a unique and memorable party setting with ease. The colors, textures, and shapes featured on the charcuterie board as well as the scrumptious desserts serve up abundant beauty.

Include fun florals to highlight or create a color scheme. They provide eye-catching height for tablescapes and background areas like shelves or mantels.

Where to put the charcuterie board? They look enticing whether they are placed on counters, kitchen tables, or bar carts. If you plan to prepare multiple trays, you can bring them out one at a time to pace the eating time; or if you're hosting a large group, size up your space to determine where the trays should go and what decor pieces can fit around them.

tip If you do the multi-tray option, be mindful of your combinations. Spread out spicy items rather than having multiples on one tray. The same goes for colors and shapes. Try to avoid piling up all your red items close together. Layer your ingredients to give your board a little depth and texture. All these tips make for a much more visually pleasing and appealing platter!

Favorite Season Picks

I hereby give you permission to play with your food. I know you've been waiting for someone to do that all your life!

ALL YOU'LL NEED: holiday-themed stickers, scrapbook paper, toothpicks. I chose pumpkin stickers to feature on our toothpicks, but you can select acorns, leaves, etc.

1. Attach the sticker to the top end of a toothpick.
2. Cut a shape from the scrapbook paper to be slightly larger than your sticker.
3. Attach it to the back side of the sticker to enclose the end of the toothpick.
4. If needed, add pieces of tape to secure.

Not only are these a fun, festive little extra feature, but they give flat foods a little height and add charm to your tablescape!

Pass the Pumpkin

Gather up the whole group to make memories and reminisce on years prior when you play Pass the Pumpkin!

Choose a plump pumpkin (artificial if you want it as a keepsake) and pass it around the group with a permanent marker. Each person shares something for which they are thankful and records it on the pumpkin. Pass the pumpkin until everyone has participated!

You might notice that last year's pumpkin is proudly perched in my tablescape mix.
See how easy it is to cultivate and celebrate new traditions?

Blessing Tree

Rally your loved ones and invite them to decorate a Thanksgiving tree. That's right. Let's bring in the green early this season. Gather the blessings and adorn your heart and home with them.

IN ADVANCE:

Select an early, small Christmas tree or bring out a member of the faux forest.

Purchase paper pieces in a variety of nature shapes such as leaves or acorns, or trim your own out of scrapbook paper. Punch a small hole at the top and add a loop of yarn or twine so that each blessing decoration can be hung with ease from a branch.

DAY OF:

Display these multicolored cutouts on a table along with glitter pens and markers.

Provide one prompt or several to keep it interesting, then invite guests to write their answer on a paper ornament and hang it up for everyone to enjoy. Here are a few ideas:

What is your favorite holiday song?

What seasonal food delights your taste buds?

Who blesses you?

What's your favorite Bible verse or saying about blessing?

Let the littles in on the action even if they can't write yet. A picture is worth a thousand words—especially when depicted by petite Picassos!

SPRINKLE IN THE SPECIAL

Spread the cheer and sprinkle in the special beyond those in your immediate family. This can be a difficult time of year for some folks. Pack up the portable food ideas in this chapter and deliver a blessing to a friend, neighbor, or someone who will be alone for the holiday season. Involve your kids or members of your church and call it a Gratitude-to-Go Gang. This might just become your favorite tradition.

Pint-Sized Pumpkin Pie

The pumpkin spice flavor you crave in a portable, adorable package.

- Jars or containers of choice
- 8 graham crackers, crumbled
- 4 T. melted butter
- 1 (8 oz.) package cream cheese, softened
- 1 cup canned pumpkin puree
- ½ cup sugar
- 1 tsp. pumpkin pie spice
- ½ tsp. vanilla extract
- 1½ cups whipped cream, divided

Combine the graham cracker crumbles and melted butter in a mixing bowl. Spoon into 8 small jars and lightly press down.

In another bowl, combine the cream cheese, pumpkin, sugar, pumpkin pie spice, and vanilla and beat until smooth. Then fold in 1 cup of whipped topping. Spoon the pumpkin filling into the jars. Top with the remaining whipped cream and serve!

Delicious Fall Dip

You'll want to dip everything you can find into this quick caramel creation!

- 1 (8 oz.) package cream cheese, softened
- Caramel sauce
- Toffee bits
- Dippers of your choice (apple slices, pretzels, graham crackers, etc.)

Simply soften your cream cheese, pour warm caramel sauce over the block, top with toffee bits, and dig in!

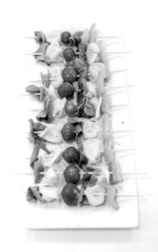

Favorite things Party

So much fun. Gather up your closest gal pals for an intimate and heartwarming experience to build community and strengthen friendships. You will get to know your girls on a deeper level and leave with a basketful of thoughtfully selected gifts. Does it get any better than that?

If you are like me, many of your must-haves came about because friends introduced you to them. This event offers the opportunity for each friend to share something they love with those they adore. From favorite lip balm or soda to the most-loved magazine or stationery set, the collected treasures will delight all. Be sure your guests know how many of their special item they need to bring so they can share with everyone. You want to be sure everyone gets their goodies.

There is a reason your friends are your friends. Are they creative and always on the lookout for good deals and special ways to celebrate life? They clearly have great taste because they love you. This party honors the bond between kindred spirits. You are going to love this time together so much. It will become one of your favorite things.

PARTY POSSIBILITIES

Pamper a dear friend with this party. Is someone facing a big life event? Is someone celebrating a milestone birthday? Invite all of your friends to bring their favorite something to the party, and gather all the treasures to give to your guest of honor. Simple gifts have great meaning when they are shared among friends. If you are hosting a housewarming, have all the guests bring their favorite home-goods item along with a note about why they love it. Your new homeowner-friend will be delighted.

Focus on the Favorites

Make sure the favorites are a focal feature to celebrate the theme. Set aside space to display the items your friends offer the group. Every special touch will go a long way in making the women you bring together feel celebrated.

For my party, I cleared off some space on the shelving in my sitting room, and it totally worked. I opted for a mobile menu of items that my girls could grab and go. Skewers worked well as part of the decor setup for the event and added splashes of color in all the right places.

I adore the vintage look of mercury glass vases in this party. Displaying your favorite things in an apothecary jar pumps up their presentation. You make a sweet connection when chitchat turns into friends sharing stories about what they brought and why it's their favorite.

tip
If your friends prefer more direction, set a theme for the favorites! The possibilities are limitless. Ask the ladies to bring their favorite hair product, nail polish, clutch, eye shadow, etc. This doesn't have to be expensive to be special.

tip
Customize this celebration to suit your guests. Choose to go extravagant or simple. Host at home or your fave hangout. As the hostess, you may wish to set an expense limit so the gifts stay simple and balanced.

I utilized several pretty trays to display and serve the skewers. I especially love featuring fresh florals to infuse the gathering spaces with fragrance and beauty. These really up the femme factor to celebrate my fave females! I also bring a Southern hospitality ambience by using a variety of blue hues.

Set Up for the Swap

This party is one big bliss activity. The conversations and laughter will flow as your friends exchange their favorite things and take delight in discovering new treasures. You can prepare for the party in four steps.

1. Prep the food.

2. Create the decor touches.

3. Craft swag baskets for the favorites swap.

4. Stylize a couple party favor favorites to initiate the fun.

SWAG BASKETS

You want your girls to gather their bounty with flair. Pick up plain baskets at your local dollar shop. Decorate each one with a whimsical, wide ribbon. Then embellish each one with friends' names or initials.

MUST-HAVE MAGAZINE

Pick up copies of the must-have magazine that tops your list. Roll the magazine into a scroll and wrap with a ribbon that reflects your style or in any color or pattern you prefer.

STATIONERY WITH A TWIST

If stationery is your jam, snag a set of spiral notebooks with cute Flair pens to match or in amazing, bright colors. Check your craft stash for washi tape and ribbon that coordinate with your colors. Tape pens to the front of the notebooks. Embellish the notebook spirals with adorable ribbon knots. Even making grocery lists will be a pleasure with this clever, pretty duo.

The Joy Exchange

Now it's time to begin the exchange. Ask someone to go first, and then work your way around the circle. Be sure everyone gets enough time to describe their favorite things and to answer any questions the others might have. Some prompts that might help each person showcase their favorites:

1. Why I was drawn to this treasure

2. How I discovered it

3. Why it is still a must-have for me

4. My hope for others as I share this favorite thing with them

Hitting pause during our busyness to discover more about the people we love, including what makes them happy, is a great practice to introduce into all of our lives.

SPRINKLE IN THE SPECIAL

This party makes me want to break out in song. Why not? It's never wrong to invite friends to start singing "My Favorite Things" in a very *Sound of Music* way. Make Julie Andrews proud, my friend! You could even start off the party by showing this famous movie scene.

Tortellini Salad Kabobs

Pasta gets a pick-me-up when layered with veggies served on a stick!

- Tortellini
- Cherry tomatoes
- Basil leaves
- Orange/red/yellow bell peppers

Cook the tortellini as directed. Slice the peppers into bite-sized chunks. Layer the ingredients onto kabob sticks and serve.

Wedge Salad Sticks

Pass on the plates with these simple and convenient salad kabob bites!

- Lettuce wedge pieces
- Cucumbers
- Carrots
- Cherry tomatoes
- Dressing

Cut the lettuce wedge into bite-sized pieces. Slice the cucumbers, carrots, and any other veggies you wish to include. Layer the items onto kabob sticks and drizzle them with your dressing of choice.

Fuss-Free Spaghetti

Forgo the fuss for simple spaghetti on a stick. This is so yummy.

- Italian meatballs (prepared)
- Spaghetti sauce (optional)
- Cooked spaghetti noodles
- Basil leaves

Warm up the meatballs as directed. You may choose to dip or soak the meatballs in the spaghetti sauce. Cook the spaghetti noodles as directed. Layer the meatballs and spin the spaghetti onto mini forks. Garnish with basil if desired.

Board Game Showdown

Move over Candy Crush—this party is bringing back the board-game tradition! Break out the classics like Bingo, Monopoly, Life, and Scrabble and show off those old-school skills. Best of all, you won't need to Risk taste and fun with this game night. It's all right here and as easy as can be to Connect your people with good times.

When the hunger games begin, your guests won't have to Go Fish. This party boasts cleverly portable snacks, which is especially helpful if you have a large group and host several game tables. Guests can move about, mingle, and cheer on players or participate, all while munching.

Divide and conquer with games like Battle of the Sexes or Beat the Parents. Who's up for a little friendly competition? Let the games begin, or you'll be ever so Sorry to miss out.

PARTY POSSIBILITIES

This is a match made in heaven for a youth or scout group party. A game-playing friend in your crowd will love this event for their birthday gathering. Make it a neighborhood event, a family vs. family competition, or a girls' night in! If you and friends watch a sport together, host this after the season is over so nobody will lose their competitive edge or the gift of regular fellowship.

Get Your Decorating Game On

This theme provides so many potential visuals for your decor. Visit a thrift store or antique shop to find used games and mine their treasures. Use game boards and checkerboards as centerpieces. Oversized checker pieces make interesting drink coasters.

Display game cards and pieces in unexpected and unusual ways. Fan out a deck of cards as a place mat under floral arrangements. Use Scrabble tiles to create name tags or food tags. If trophies are created ahead of time, you definitely want to display those front and center so everyone can see the pretty prizes.

Designate game hub locations by age group or type. For example, kids' games in the kitchen or active games (like Twister) in the living room. Decorate those areas with relevant elements. For the Twister example, you could tape large construction paper circles in red, yellow, and blue to echo the game mat.

Give your floral arrangements a winning touch. Insert a cylinder-shaped flower vase into an apothecary jar. Sandwich the domino pieces in between the two and add your favorite fresh flowers to the vase.

tip Instead of supplying all the games and snacks yourself, ask the guests to each bring their favorite game so that you have a variety of options. If you are celebrating a particular person, be sure their favorite game is represented.

Mason Jar Trophy

This do-in-advance DIY will become someone's prized possession. These are simple to create, so you can easily make a trove of trophies to present to every participant. Or show a competitive spirit and award a couple trophies based on points and scores and best attitude.

By the way, once guests see these clever trophies, you will win Best Hostess, so you had better make one for yourself!

ALL YOU'LL NEED: mason jars, mini plastic trophies, spray paint in any color (consider metallic), hot glue gun

1. Spray paint the trophies and let them dry.

2. Hot glue each trophy base onto the top of a mason jar lid.

3. Fill the mason jars with yummy treats.

4. Screw on the tops.

5. Present to the happy winners.

SPRINKLE IN THE SPECIAL

Even old-school games can get a new age makeover! Pull out your old Jenga set from the closet and add a little flair by attaching washi tape to the end of the blocks. Mix your patterns and colors to make it extra funky. Use this as a centerpiece for the kids' table.

Veggie Cups

Don't stress the mess with these all-in-one veggie cups.

- Peppers
- Cucumbers
- Carrots
- Celery
- Ranch dressing

Slice the veggies into strips or sticks. Pour ranch dressing into the bottom of cups. Add veggie sticks to the cups and serve.

To-Go Tacos

Tuck your favorite taco ingredients in a personal bag of tortilla chips.

- Individual bags of tortilla chips
- Ground beef
- Taco seasoning
- Shredded cheese of choice
- Shredded lettuce
- Chopped cherry tomatoes
- Additional favorite taco fixin's: peppers, tomatillos, mango salsa, chopped onions

Prepare the ground beef with the taco seasoning and place it in a bowl. Set out the taco toppings buffet style. Cut along the long sides of each personal-sized tortilla chip bag. Hand these off to the guests so they can add the beef and sprinkle on their taco toppers. No plates, no mess, and a whole lot of fun.

Walking S'mores

Your game face isn't complete without that sweet tooth. Walking S'mores satisfy the sugar craving with convenience.

- Teddy Graham snack packs
- Mini marshmallows (estimate ¼ cup per bag)
- Milk chocolate bars, chopped (estimate ½ bar per bag)

Cut open the snack packs so they don't tear. Add the chocolate chunks. Broil the marshmallows until golden brown. Divide the toasted marshmallows between the snack packs. Shake the bags to combine the ingredients. Enjoy with a fork.

Merry & Bright

Deck the halls with wows and jolly laughter as you wrap your home, friends, and gifts in the holiday spirit. Hosting a Christmas party might seem like a very big addition for the season, but I'll make sure your tinsel doesn't get in a tangle. In fact, what if the party actually moved a few things *off* your to-do list? I think I just made your holiday brighter, right? This is a wrapping party. A get-it-done-and-have-fun afternoon.

Be prepared to make everyone's nice list. Invite girlfriends, neighbors, or church groups for an event yule all enjoy. Sharing time and making memories while putting together pretty packages for loved ones or those in need will sleigh any crowd. Your guests will be so thankful to get ahead of the Christmas crunch as they pause and enjoy the company of friends.

This party is decked out with snacks, sweets, crafts, and gifts, so be sure to take an elfie to post on snow-cial media! I'm sprinkling merry and just-right ideas here, so you don't have to go Grinch when planning and prepping.

PARTY POSSIBILITIES

Gather up the gals in your charity group to wrap gifts for underprivileged families. Make a day of it with a morning trip to the mall to select tags with holiday wishes from the giving trees, followed by an afternoon of shopping and then wrapping. Moms of Girl Scouts can get the troop together to package presents for soldiers. Local schools may offer up wish lists from students with needs that your prayer group could craft contributions for.

Adorn We Now Our Sleigh Table Apparel

Dress up your tables with decor that is festive and functional. I created sleigh stations to showcase the holiday theme and to organize our gift-wrapping supplies. Tabletop Christmas trees of various heights add dimension and visual delight.

White tableware works for every occasion, but don't be afraid to throw in some fun holiday prints and patterns. Are you someone who collects Christmas plate sets? Mix and match to create a clever display.

Personalize the party spaces with your favorite holiday treasures and centerpieces. What makes your home merry and bright? Maybe it's white ceramic angels or a family keepsake manger. It could be an eclectic mix of colors and patterns presented in the tablecloth, runner, and napkins.

tip This party theme is portable enough to bring the cheer anywhere. If you are sharing this event with coworkers, break out the party in the breakroom. Need to keep the gifts out of sight of little wandering eyes? Coordinate with friends to meet when kiddos are at soccer practice, or simply gather in a more secluded space like the basement or bonus room.

Wreath Wrapping

Even if your paper is plain, you can beat the blah by throwing unexpected objects into the mix, like a mini grapevine wreath.

ALL YOU'LL NEED: wide ribbon in a couple colors, tape, small grapevine wreaths from a craft store, artificial flowers

1. Take two long strands of wide ribbon and tape one end of each to the back of the gift.

2. Flip the box over.

3. Lay a small grapevine wreath on the top of the gift.

4. Thread each strand of wide ribbon through the top and bottom of the wreath.

5. Tape the strands to the back so the grapevine wreath is suspended by the ribbons.

6. Add artificial flowers.

Wrap Outside the Box!

Personalize presents with custom-crafted bows and tags that really provide a personal touch! Have your friends bring over their stash of presents to wrap, or plan to wrap gifts for certain groups, like teachers and pastors or organizations that deliver presents to kids in need.

Pom-Poms and Beads

Embellish with style. Any package looks like a million bucks when we add texture and sparkle with beads and poms.

ALL YOU'LL NEED: beads and yarn (or premade poms) in a variety of colors, glue

1. Have your guests choose colors that complement or contrast the wrapping paper they are using.

2. Glue the beads to the packages.

3. Personalize the gifts with alphabet beads that spell the recipients' names.

4. Add the perfect pom pop of color. Purchase them premade, or follow your favorite tutorial (see page 151) to make your own. Want to go really simple? Wrap yarn multiple times around gifts to pump up the presentation factor.

SPRINKLE IN THE SPECIAL

Plan for a paper potluck! Ask your guests to bring extra wrapping paper, ribbon, bows, stickers, and sparkly extras they have tucked away in their craft stash so everyone can share and swap. Check out the variety of colors and patterns the group can work with now! Be bold as you mix paper designs: solids, stripes with polka dots, patterned ribbons, plaid bows.

Santa's Stamp Shop

Everyone will be impressed with this craft. It helps that it's a Noel no-brainer because your guests get to leave the party with an actual present or two. What? Santa's stamp shop lets them create personalized gifts and tags made with a basic leather stamping set. If you don't have a kit, ask around to borrow one from a friend who has a set in her craft closet.

ALL YOU'LL NEED: leather tags and bracelets, stamp kit, ideas!

IN ADVANCE:

Purchase the number of blank leather bracelets and tags you'll need. I like to have enough for everyone to create one piece of jewelry and one tag. You might even want to let guests know about this activity in advance so they can bring any extra leather pieces they'd like to turn into something special.

DAY OF:

Review the directions that accompany the kit you'll use. Our gathering for this party used mallets and alphabet stamps to imprint leather strands with friends' names or warmhearted phrases. I'm not sure when I've had so much fun creating one-of-a-kind gifts and prettifying packages. Suggest verse references, happy words and phrases, or nicknames as possible bracelet impressions.

Pomegranate Party Dip

Less time in the kitchen means more time making memories when you work a little holiday magic on a traditional favorite to whip up this dip.

- 3 medium, ripe avocados
- 2 T. lime juice
- ¼ cup red onion, diced
- ¼ cup cilantro, chopped
- 1 jalapeño (seeds removed and minced)
- Salt and pepper
- 1 cup pomegranate arils
- Kosher salt and black pepper to taste

Slicing from top to bottom, cut the avocados in half and remove the pit. Spoon the good stuff into a medium-sized bowl.

Add the remaining ingredients except the pomegranate. Mash the mixture until you've reached the desired consistency. Season with salt and black pepper to taste.

Finally, stir in the pomegranate arils. Serve with tortilla chips.

Strawberry Santa Hats

Be prepared for a round of Santa-plause when guests dive into these sweet Santa hats. These tasty bites are a real Christmas miracle as they come together with only three ingredients!

- Strawberries (hulled)
- Oreos
- Cream cheese frosting (premade or homemade)

Add a dollop of cream cheese frosting to the top of each cookie. Place the strawberry hulled-side down onto the frosting and press gently to secure in place. Pipe or place a dot of frosting on the tip of the strawberry for the ball on the Santa hat. Enjoy!

Festive Fruit Pizza

This festive fresh-fruit wreath is incredibly appetizing, and it doubles as a holiday decor accent!

- 1 (16.5 oz.) tube of refrigerated sugar cookie dough
- 1 (8 oz.) package cream cheese, softened
- ⅓ cup granulated sugar
- 2 T. milk
- ½ tsp. vanilla extract
- 1 to 2 tsp. lemon or lime juice
- Fresh fruit of your liking (we love raspberries, blueberries, and strawberries)
- Fresh mint to garnish

Preheat your oven per the directions on your cookie dough.

Grease your pizza pan and then spread the cookie dough evenly on the pizza pan in the shape of a ring. (You might use a small bowl as a template for the center of your ring if desired. Or wing it!) Bake per the directions. In a mixing bowl, combine the cream cheese, sugar, milk, vanilla, and lime juice.

Remove the cookie-crust ring from the oven and set it out to cool. Once it is cooled completely, spread the cream cheese mixture on the top. Add fruit as toppings on your cookie-crust pizza. Place fresh mint as a garnish to complete the wreath look.

about THE AUTHOR

BRITTANY YOUNG has spent years sharing entertainment tips and tricks to make celebrations easier to organize and follow through with on her website and online community, *Certified Celebrator*. Through articles, tutorials, and posts on her various social media channels, Young encourages readers by providing doable and manageable pointers for hosting memorable social gatherings and celebrations while remaining budget friendly and time efficient.

CONNECT WITH BRITTANY

@certifiedcelebrator

facebook.com/certifiedcelebrator

www.certifiedcelebrator.com

The Team at Certified Celebrator

I hope that behind every hardworking boss-mama sprinkled with success is a team of soul sisters who encourage and inspire her as much as these wonder women empower and support me in my effervescent endeavors every single day!

JENNIFER MOWRY, CREATIVE DIRECTOR

Jennifer and I work closely together creating content for brands, the blog, videos, and this book! Jennifer leads the vision and guides every event, project, and party through each step of our process till the very end. She plans and develops anywhere from three to six creative projects a week.

Jennifer "Fancy Pants" Mowry is 100 percent responsible for maintaining my sanity and keeping me on track for long-term goals.

JULIE HALL, PHOTOGRAPHER

Introducing Julie Hall of Julie Hall Photography (aka the Certified Celebrator Photo Pro). Julie is the magician—she has the best tips and tricks up her sleeve. Always capturing angles and moments that somehow make us look pretty and put-together even on our craziest, most hot-mess days is nothing short of magic. She keeps us creatives on track, dialing us back in so we can take advantage of the best light while we've got it. But don't misunderstand—she is always up for a little old-school rap music throw down. Word!

CASEY BATES, COPYWRITER AND SCHEDULE KEEPER

Casey is the master and maker of our Certified Celebrator written content. She is the pen behind the blog, newsletter, mini mag, and anything else requiring words. I have the gift of gab, and I can chat with you all day, but writing is not my jam. Casey has a way of transcribing our crazy audio notes and simple photos into content that not only communicates our goals but always makes us sound smart (and sassy!). She was the very first employee of Certified Celebrator, and I swear to you it was one of the best decisions I've ever made.

AMY GRACE, STYLIST

Amy Grace (aka The Sandy Pearls) is our certified stylist! She steps on the scene with her sassy swagger and helps each of us put our best foot forward with style. She understands the brand and styles us in pieces that dress us in confidence to help us find our best self. Incorporating tiny touches that require little to no effort is her strong suit. One of her key comments when an outfit doesn't display our best features is "Girl, that does nothing for you." See? Even that is delivered with a positive vibe. Amy is our confidence coach; without her, we would lack the sass factor.

KRISTA JACKSON, BRAND DEVELOPER AND ILLUSTRATOR

Krista works diligently to develop our brand with catchy, cute graphics and illustrations. She pours her heart and soul into our monthly digital magazine *Celebrate with Sprinkles*. It's nothing short of a miracle how she manages to take my head-in-the-clouds visions and turn them into amazing graphics and dreamy doodles. All of our tags and wallpapers are Krista's creative inventions, and we have officially crowned her the Princess of Printables!

ANDREA UHLENHOPP, COLLABORATIONS COORDINATOR

Andrea works closely with interesting and exciting brands to connect their message to our loyal followers, broadening our celebration to include even more creative lines and products. She builds collaborative partnerships that expand our outreach and increase the population of people engaged in and passionate about intentionally celebrating their loved ones! Andrea keeps us accountable with her timelines and to-do lists. She is the Diva of Deadlines!

Unless otherwise indicated, all Scripture quotations are taken from the Holy Bible, New International Version®, NIV®. Copyright © 1973, 1978, 1984, 2011 by Biblica, Inc.® Used by permission. All rights reserved worldwide.

Verses marked NLT are taken from the Holy Bible, New Living Translation, copyright © 1996, 2004, 2015 by Tyndale House Foundation. Used by permission of Tyndale House Publishers, Inc., Carol Stream, Illinois 60188. All rights reserved.

Cover and interior design by Faceout Studio
Photography by Julie Hall
Hand-lettering and illustrations by Krista Jackson

Celebrate with Sprinkles
Copyright © 2020 by Brittany Young
Published by Harvest House Publishers
Eugene, Oregon 97408
www.harvesthousepublishers.com

ISBN 978-0-7369-7903-0 (Hardcover)

Library of Congress Cataloging-in-Publication Data Record is available at https://lccn.loc.gov/2019054616

Printed in China

20 21 22 23 24 25 26 27 28 / RP-FO/ 10 9 8 7 6 5 4 3